A *Life*
of Faith

FROM WEST AFRICA TO HER
AMERICAN DREAM

MAI C. STEVENS

ISBN 978-1-0980-7261-2 (paperback)
ISBN 978-1-0980-7262-9 (hardcover)
ISBN 978-1-0980-7263-6 (digital)

Christian Faith Publishing, Inc.
832 Park Avenue
Meadville, PA 16335
www.christianfaithpublishing.com

Printed in the United States of America

This book is dedicated to my daughter Honey Makrah
who left this world before her second birthday.

Chapter 1

Childhood

The lessons were challenging at Cavalla School in rural Liberia, West Africa. It was approaching graduation time. Faith and her fellow senior classmates were excitedly looking forward to graduating from sixth grade and moving on to junior high school located in Harper, the main city. However, in order to graduate, students had to take and pass two major exams. Faith and her cousin, Budu, who was also her classmate, studied hard and excelled academically, passing the exams with flying colors.

All new graduates in her neighborhood were preparing to go to boarding schools in the main city. It was an exciting time for all of them. Those in the "in-group" were hoping that all of them would be leaving together for junior high school. Faith believed she was a member of the in-group because Mama held a high-ranking position as a schoolteacher. Most of the in-group students were children of staff members, who held high positions within the city.

Faith watched Mama as she prepared Budu for boarding school. Many of their friends' parents were also getting them ready. She waited anxiously for Mama to finish packing Budu's belongings to get to hers. She could not wait. They had grown up together as biological siblings, receiving the same training and nurturing from their parents, without any distinction being made between them.

So all their friends were expecting that they would be leaving home together for boarding school.

However, to Faith's utter surprise, Budu left for boarding school without her. And to add to her distress, everyone in her circle of friends also left. She was the only one left behind. Not understanding and wondering how this could happen to her, she cried bitterly. Mama and Dada had always treated Budu and her equally, so why were they treating her differently now? And because they were not offering her any explanation for their unfair decision, she was confused, disappointed, and frustrated. Without saying anything, she quietly packed some of her things and left Mama and Dada Paul's home. She knew that this setback did not support her dream of going to America. Even though she had no idea, at that point, how her dream would become a reality.

At the early age of ten, Faith overheard some older women talking about Mrs. Finley. They said she was a well-educated and influential Liberian woman, who gained status in society because she was educated in the United States of America. From that day, Faith had a burning desire to become like Mrs. Finley, and her dream of going to American was born. It became her drive, the thing she vowed to pursue! So she worked diligently to nurture and protect her "American dream" from all naysayers, including her best friends, siblings, and even her parents. All of them ridiculed and considered her as being silly for dreaming such an impossible dream. She, therefore, built a mental fortress around her dream and promised herself that even abject poverty would not prevent her from accomplishing it.

However, a few years later, Faith's greatest fear became a reality. It shattered the foundation of her faith and left her teetering on the brink of hopelessness, wondering whether she would ever attain her dream of going to America. That was when Mama and Dada, the only parents she knew, who had always shown no distinction between Budu and her, sent Budu off to boarding school without her. She felt so rejected. It was difficult understanding her parents' decision not to send her with Budu to boarding school. At this point, the only thing Faith could think about was to leave home and ventured out into the world in pursuit of her dream.

Who was Faith and where did she come from?

Faith was born in Cavalla Firestone Hospital in Maryland County, Liberia, where her mother, Ms. Scott, worked. She was Ms. Scott's third child and the only child of her father, Mr. Lewis. Her mother was from Cape Palmas, Maryland County, and her father was from Monrovia, Montserrado County. Mr. Lewis relocated from Monrovia to a town in Liberia called Buah where he owned a large farm, growing rice, rubber, cocoa, and different kinds of fruits and vegetables. He had a cousin who also relocated from Monrovia to Maryland to work for Cavalla Firestone Plantation. His name was Mr. Paul. Mr. Lewis visited his cousin occasionally. On one of his visits, Mr. Lewis met Ms. Scott. They began communicating and developed a serious relationship; they fell in love, giving birth to Faith.

When Faith was almost a year old, one of her mother's friends, named Mother Annie, watched her friend struggle to care for her infant baby girl and two other children. She was so moved by her friend's inability to care for three children, she decided to step in and offer her help. Mother Annie told Faith's mother that she would like to take Faith to live with her in Harper. She promised that she would provide well for the baby and give her the best of care as she had no children of her own to care for. Ms. Scott was taken aback and overwhelmed with emotions. She knew how difficult life was for her, a single mother with three children, and she imagined that Faith would have opportunities that she was unable to give her. She was confident that she could entrust her baby's care to her good friend, but even so, she was somewhat indecisive. But after much contemplation with mixed emotions of sadness that her baby would be leaving her and gratitude that her good friend wanted to provide for her baby what she was clearly unable to give her, she agreed to have Mother Annie take care of her baby girl. Mother Annie was so elated to have Faith. She loved her and was devoted to giving her the best care she could. However, this arrangement was short-lived.

One day, Faith's father, Mr. Lewis, who was not involved in her day-to-day upkeep because he lived very far on his farm, sent one of his farmworkers, Boimah, to deliver supplies for Faith. Faith's mother, Ms. Scott, accepted the supplies but mentioned to Boimah that Faith was now living with her friend, Mother Annie, in Harper. And so he went back to the farm and reported to Mr. Lewis that his baby daughter was no longer with her mother but lived with her friend in Harper. Mr. Lewis was furious to hear this news. He immediately left his farm and went to Mother Annie's home to get Faith. This was a very traumatic experience for Mother Annie, who had formed a strong bond with Faith. She grieved the separation but could do nothing about it.

Although Mr. Lewis lived on his farm, he did not want Faith living on a farm. There were no schools in proximity of the farm. And the ones that were farther away, he did not think were good enough. He decided that Faith would do well in an environment like Cavalla where his cousin, Mr. Paul, lived with his family. Mr. Paul and his wife had six children, who were all grown and had left home except for two. They were now rearing two of their grandchildren, who were similar in age to Faith. He had no doubt that they would agree to accept Faith in their home and help her get the kind of education she would need for future success. Cavalla was a modern city with electricity and running water, and the elementary school was the best in the area.

Most people, who lived on farms in villages, had no electricity, running water, and good schools. So they brought their children to live in the city with people who could provide access to good education and proper home training. This was a common practice in Liberia. These children helped with household chores and worked well. Their parents wanted them to receive a good education and proper home training. Many of them appreciated the opportunity and did whatever was necessary to fulfill their parents' good intentions for their future. And so they worked hard to excel. Most of them succeeded and made their parents proud.

And so Faith's father took her to live with his cousin, Mr. Paul, and his wife, affectionately called Dada and Mama, after they had agreed to become her guardians. Dada and Mama were also taking care of two of their grandchildren, Jeanne and Budu, who were of the same age as Faith, all preschoolers. They were all enrolled in Cavalla School, where Mama was a teacher. Faith fitted in well with Mama and Dada and her cousins, Jeanne and Budu. She enjoyed the same treatment and privileges in Mama and Dada's home as her cousins. After a while, Faith's father, seeing how well his cousin and his wife were taking care of his daughter, arranged with them to have Faith's younger brother, Lewellyn, live with them as well. Mama and Dada were good people. They didn't mind helping their cousin with his children because he was family, and family help family. They knew he was grateful to them and showed it in many ways. Mr. Lewis appreciated their help and was doing his part to care for his children.

Faith couldn't be happier to have her younger brother and cousins living together as all siblings, celebrating and enjoying birthdays and holidays together. Her mama was a great seamstress. She made beautiful outfits and taught many women in the neighborhood as well how to sew. Faith and her peers sometimes went to children's dances and movies at the clubhouse, dressed in beautiful clothes Mama had tirelessly made. Her childhood was full of unforgettable moments of an enjoyable life with Mama and Dada. They were her parents as a child. She saw her biological parents only occasionally.

Mama received her bachelor's in education from the University of Liberia. She was a true educator, and every child who came to live with her attended Cavalla Elementary School. She was also a disciplinarian, and the training that she and Dada gave prepared all who lived with them, including Faith, to cope with future life experiences.

However, Faith was having a hard time dealing with the disappointment of not being allowed to attend boarding school in Harper. And even though she was still a young girl, her only thought was to leave Dada and Mama's home because she didn't feel welcomed there anymore. She couldn't believe what had just happened to her. Facing a predicament, she wished she had somewhere else to go instead of to her biological mother's home. Not having spent much time with her, she barely knew her. But on the other hand, she reminded herself that she thought she knew Mama and Dada well. She had spent almost all her life with them, and they had cared for her and treated her well until now. And here she was devastated because they broke her trust and belief that she was an equally important member of their family. She just couldn't figure out why the sudden rejection.

And even worse, they were not giving her any reason for their decision nor consolation, knowing how badly their decision was affecting her.

Feeling sad and lonely, Faith quietly left Cavalla without Mama and Dada's knowledge and went to her biological mother's home in a not-too-distant town called Plebo. It was painful leaving her peers behind in Cavalla, and getting adjusted to living with her mother was also a challenge. However, just two weeks after she arrived at her mother's home, news came that her great-grandmother, Ma Wede who lived in Harper had died. Faith and her mother, as well as many other family members, traveled from their homes in Plebo, Monrovia and other towns to Harper to attend her funeral. During this time, Faith met some new relatives and others she barely knew.

After the funeral, one of her cousins on her mother's side named Annabel suggested to Faith's mother that she should let Faith live with her in Monrovia, where she would get to meet other members of her father's family. This would be her third move. However, she was very excited about the prospects of living in a large more modern city and getting acquainted with new family members. So shortly after her great-grandmother's funeral, she and her mother exchanged goodbyes, and then she flew to Monrovia with her Cousin Annabel.

Life in Monrovia

Schools in Monrovia were basically classified into four main groups: public schools, private schools, private boarding schools, and night schools. Public schools were government-funded schools, which cater mostly to the general public at little or no fees to students. The standard of education at some of these schools was lower than that of private schools. Whereas private schools were run mainly by private organizations or individuals with little or no subsidies from the government. The standard of education at these schools was perceived to be higher, as well as tuitions. Only students with working parents and those with scholarships could afford to attend these schools. On the other hand, private boarding schools were also run by private entities, providing home and learning for students away from home. These schools were mostly unaffordable by most parents due to high tuitions and boarding fees. The standard of education here was also considered higher and desirable by working parents. And night schools generally catered to working adults who had not completed high school due to dropouts or other reasons but found it necessary later to get a high school diploma. These schools were both publicly and privately operated.

Upon arrival in Monrovia, Cousin Annabel had Faith enrolled in a private school named Harris School. Faith was studious and did well in her lessons. She was very happy and grateful that her cousin could afford the costs of private school for her. Soon, she began to feel comfortable in her new environment and made new friends. The loneliness and longing for her friends that she initially experienced after leaving Cavalla were no longer profound. As she began to mingle with other students at school and in her neighborhood, she ran into a young lady named Bernice, who had the same last name as hers, Lewis. Faith was immediately curious because she had not heard of anyone else with her last name, except for her siblings who lived in Maryland County, where she grew up. She told Bernice that her father's name was Abraham Lewis, and then Bernice told her that she had an uncle with the same name. They were both excited about the possibility of being related. Bernice then asked Faith to wait a few minutes after school so she could introduce her to her father, who was picking her up. To their amazement, Bernice's father turned out to be Faith's uncle, Ben Lewis, and he was clearly delighted to meet her. He told her she resembled her father and mentioned that her father had informed him about her move to Monrovia and wanted him to look for her.

Since Faith moved to Monrovia to live with her cousin Annabel, her father had been worried about her. And so he was very happy and relieved when his brother informed him of their chanced meeting. Faith's uncle Ben, came to visit her at Cousin Annabel's home and was pleased with what he saw. Annabel lived in a decent neighborhood, and Faith was being well cared for. A week later, Uncle Ben returned to visit Faith his niece and gave her some money. It happened that the Lewis' family sold some of their property and divided the proceeds among themselves, and Faith's father decided to send a portion of his share for her tuition. Mr. Lewis told her that her dad was pleased to know he was in touch with her, and he promised he would come to visit her soon. Eventually, Faith discovered that all her father's relatives lived in Monrovia, except for Dada, who was the only one she knew and had lived with in Cavalla.

While Faith was getting adjusted to life in Monrovia, living with Cousin Annabel, enjoying school, and making new friends, she was unaware of challenges to come. Her cousin Annabel and her boyfriend, Mr. Lee, a well-known man, had a baby named Leroy.

Whenever Mr. Lee came to visit, he would ask Faith to ride along with him and Leroy to buy ice cream. To her amazement, Mr. Lee would always try to touch her in an inappropriate, sexual manner on the trips to buy ice cream. And she always screamed. She couldn't understand Mr. Lee's intention and despicable behavior. This was upsetting to her because Mama and Dada had instilled in her good moral values in a well-disciplined home. And so she did not expect that kind of behavior from an older man, especially one who was Cousin Annabel's friend. She hated his assaults but was afraid to tell Cousin Annabel because she was unsure how she would react if she told her. While deciding what to do about the embarrassing situation she found herself in, she recalled conversations she had been involved in with friends at school when sexual harassment affecting young women was being discussed. She learned that it was not a topic that was addressed at home or within the community. In fact, it was widely accepted and considered a prestigious thing for young women to date older men of high status, whether they were married or not. Her friends warned that young girls talking about sexual harassment at home or around town would create animosity and label them as troublemakers.

Nevertheless, Faith was conflicted, facing a predicament and not really knowing what to do. She did not know how to avoid Mr. Lee's despicable sexual advances, nor did she know who to talk to about it. Discussing this with one of her friends, Edith, did not provide any advice on how to handle the situation. Because older men's sexual abuse was such a common occurrence among young girls, it seemed to be the norm that nobody took seriously. Faith often wondered why Cousin Annabel always let her accompany Mr. Lee and their baby when there were others in the home who could have gone with him to buy ice cream. She was curious whether her cousin was aware of this problem faced by young girls or even if she knew what Mr. Lee was doing to her. Was she condoning what Mr. Lee was doing because she didn't want him to leave her? Of course, he was a good provider, and she probably needed his help. Whatever the case, Faith was very worried about what was going on as she had never experienced that kind of disrespect or harassment before. And no one had given her warning that this could happen to her or how to handle it.

When her mother relocated to Monrovia some time later, Faith felt relieved, believing that she would get counseling and advise about how to handle Mr. Lee. It was an opportunity to have a face-to-face conversation with her mother about what was happening to her at Cousin Annabel's house. She felt she could rely on her to understand her dilemma and advise her appropriately. And so one day, after her school's parade, she visited her mother to let her know about the embarrassing situation she was facing at Cousin Annabel's home. She sat down with her mother and explained every detail about Mr. Lee's inappropriate sexual advances toward her. Afterward, she immediately felt a rush of relief, having poured out her heart and all her stifled frustration. She was relying on her mother to give her an advice that would work, one that would end her frustration and put her mind at ease. But to her utter disbelief, her mother offered absolutely no advice. Heartbroken and disappointed, she came to the realization that her mother had to have knowledge about the sexual abuse young girls were subjected by older men. And, she probably experienced it herself as a young girl. She reasoned that her mother gave her no advice because she didn't want her to lose the opportunities and help her cousin was able to provide her. And so she assumed that her mother's silence was a suggestion to her that she should also keep quiet and learn to cope with Mr. Lee's unwanted and embarrassing sexual advances.

The meeting with her mother did not last long. So when she got home, Cousin Annabel asked why she had not come home immediately after her school parade. Faith told her that she went to see her mother. To her surprise, Cousin Annabel became furious and told her to pack her belongings and leave her house immediately. She was completely taken aback because she had not spent a very long time with her mother. And she could not understand why Cousin Annabel would be so upset about her going to see her mother at all. This made her sad and worried because she knew her mother could not support her nor afford her private school tuition. Amid her sadness, she found relief. The problem with Mr. Lee that she had been searching for a solution for suddenly came to an end. She would no longer be touched by his dirty, filthy hands.

After Faith left Cousin Annabel's home, she moved in with her mother who lived in a single room with her other three children. This was Faith's fourth move. The neighborhood was fine, but her mother was struggling to support her children and herself at the mercy of a few relatives who gave her occasional help. Her mother recently moved to Monrovia, hoping for a better life. Unfortunately, she saw her hopes fizzling out as her search for employment proved unsuccessful. Faith had nowhere else to live but with her mother and three siblings in a single congested room. It was difficult adjusting as she had never lived under such stringent conditions before. They barely had any food and practically had to fend for themselves. As her mother's ability to support her family remained challenging, Faith worried about her future.

Teen Years

Because Faith's mother was barely able to provide for her family, she was in no position to afford Faith's tuition at the private school she attended while living with Cousin Annabel. And there was no assistance coming from her father. It was the norm during this time for young teenage girls like her to find a way to take care of themselves and sometimes their families when the parents were unable to do so. Even some of her friends were hustling to provide for their families by dating older working men who would provide for their upkeep. It was a commonplace for these men, married or not, to seduce young girls who relied on them for their livelihood. Faith was not used to such a life because Mama and Dada had taken care of her and provided all her needs when she lived with them, just as they did their own children.

Without funds for tuition at the private school she was attending, Faith had to transfer to her neighborhood public school. It was easy for her to walked to and from school. She made many friends and became acquainted with some relatives in her neighborhood. And one of her mother's cousins, Alvina, did not live far from them. She visited her often and sometimes enjoyed meals at her home when there was no food at her mother's place. She also found moral support there, and life seemed good.

When Faith heard that her cousin Dada was in town from Harper where he and Mama lived after retiring from Cavalla, she was very excited and did not hesitate to visit him. Even though she still regretted his and Mama's decision not to send her to boarding school, she, however, remembered how well they treated her when she lived with them. And so she wanted to see Dada, who had come to Monrovia to attend his sister, Cousin Laura's funeral. It was a sad occasion for Dada, but he was also excited to see Faith again. During their visit, Dada asked her to come dressed in black the next day to attend Cousin Laura's funeral with him. After the funeral, she stayed with Dada for a while at Cousin Laura's house. She had no idea that would be the last time she saw him because he died shortly after he returned home to Harper.

Later during the year, Mama felt the need to take time away from grieving the loss of her husband, Dada. She came to Monrovia to spend time with her daughter, Princess. Faith visited her, and they were happy to see each other. During their time together, Mama used the opportunity to share some priceless wisdom about being a young woman with Faith.

"Faith, I think this is the right time for me to share some thoughts with you," Mama began.

"About what? About whom, Mama?"

"About boys. Yes, the fresh boys who think they are men, but they are still boys, wet behind the ears."

"What about them, Mama?"

"Watch out for them. They would ruin you and go on to ruin many more young girls, if they let them. You see, they would play with you and impregnate you, if you let them. And I am advising you, my child, don't let them play with you until they have earned the right to do so. If you must, and nature demands that women bear children, pick a young man who has his head on right."

"His head on right?"

"My child, I mean he should be committed and very devoted to you and family. Make sure you distinguish a good man from a bad one. A man with his upper head on right is a man who has the means to take care of his children. He does not blindly scatter babies all over creation like litters and not take care of them. Marry a good man with a sound disciplined mind. Never have baby by any man before marriage. The carnal rule is marriage before making babies."

"I am enjoying your lecture, Mama, and I want you to tell me more."

"I have told you enough. I have given you a piece of wisdom that will sustain you in life, if you live by it. I know I reared you well, and I believe you will become a successful woman. God bless you."

"Thank you so much, Mama."

Faith then hugged Mama goodbye. She realized that even though Mama had aged, she was still the same very wise and strict disciplinarian she remembered her to be. She was truly the caliber of woman that Faith wanted to emulate. Unfortunately, that was the last time Faith saw her mama. She also died shortly after she returned home to Harper. Faith's dada and mama died less than a year apart.

Although Faith had not left Dada and Mama's home in Cavalla on good terms, she could not forget their kindness to her, especially during her formative childhood years. They had given her the same nurturing, love, care, and attention that they gave their grandson, Budu. Besides their decision to send Budu to junior high school in Harper, without affording her the same privilege, she could not recall any other time when she felt overlooked while in their care. They had loved her as their own child, and she had loved them as her real parents. And this was the reason why Faith was so devastated when she was unable to attend her mama and dada's funerals.

Even though she worked for a church at the time, she could not afford to travel to Harper for neither of their funerals. Faith cried inconsolably at their loss. She recalled that all through her hard times in Monrovia, she did not get a visit from any of her cousins with whom she had grown up. They never invited her to any of the family functions. It seemed like they did not care whether she lived or died. She felt as if she had grown up with no relatives. And hardship seemed to wipe away all the good memories she ever had about growing up with Dada and Mama in Cavalla.

After years of Faith's father not being physically involved in her life, he suddenly felt the need to travel from his farm in rural parts to

Monrovia to see her, as well as other family members. She was happy to see her father when she visited him at her uncle Ben's house. And he was very happy to see her as well. However, she noticed that he did not look very well. And shortly afterward, he was admitted to a hospital in Monrovia where he unfortunately died. She struggled to understand what was happening; her world seemed to be tumbling upside down. The little bit of hope she had that her father's coming to town would be the end of her hardship suddenly vanished. She was once again devastated.

In the meantime, her mother, still struggling to establish a better living arrangement for her family, decided to move from the inner city to her longtime friend Velma's home, located on the outskirts of the city in an area called Douala. However, she could only afford to rent a single room in her friend's home. Again, Faith experienced another move for the fifth time, but their living arrangement remained the same. They all still had to share a single room. Faith had known her mother's friend, Ma Velma, since her childhood when she lived with Mama and Dada in Cavalla. Ma Velma and her family then lived in the same subdivision as Mama and Dada, and her children and Faith knew each other well. At the time, Faith's mother lived in another town called Plebo. Faith was happy to be with Ma Velma and her children, but she missed her family and friends in the inner city.

Taking Care of Herself

Moving away from the inner city to the suburbs created a hardship for Faith attending school. The public school she attended was no longer in walking distance. And without money for public transportation, getting to school became very difficult. The fact was her mother was unable to provide for her, and there was no one else who could help. At this point, Faith knew she had to find a way to take care of herself. Ma Velma's daughter, Caroline, who was friendly with Faith, also attended the same public school as Faith. And so they traveled to school together. Even though Ma Velma would give Caroline money for transportation, Faith unfortunately often did not have money for transportation. So Caroline joined her in begging their friends for money to help. In addition, on many occasions when they returned from school, Caroline was kind to share her meals with her so she wouldn't go hungry. Faith's mother was having a difficult time even providing daily meals for her children. And there were many days when she had nothing prepared for them to eat. Faith found her family's situation very pitiful and embarrassing, but she was a young lady and unable to help. She had to endure the embarrassment of begging or go without.

As things seemed to be settling for Faith and her family at Ma Velma's home, she was feeling very grateful to Ma Velma and her family for their many acts of kindness to them. She was adjusting to the neighborhood and making new friends. However, one day, Faith returned home from school only to have her mother tell her that she was moving back to the inner city. This was very surprising news for her because she thought things were going well. And it made her so sad to leave Ma Velma and her family who had helped her greatly. She also didn't want to leave Caroline and the new friends she had made in the neighborhood. But once again, Faith had no choice; she had to leave with her mother since she was still dependent on her for what little help she could give.

Relocating back into the heart of Monrovia, Faith's sixth move, this neighborhood was new to her and her siblings. Already, she was feeling a sense of great loss, loss of the good people, Ma Velma and her family, especially her dear friend and schoolmate, Caroline. She could not imagine finding anyone so willing to step in and help her as they did during the times when her mother had nothing. She knew no one in her new neighborhood, and she dreaded making new friends. She hated leaving her friends behind every time they had to move from one place to another. It wasn't long before she realized that the private school she attended when she lived with Cousin Annabel was just a few blocks away. She was sad being so close to the school that she loved so much but could not attend. Her mother just could not afford the tuition and other fees. She missed her former friends at this school, and it was difficult for her living nearby but too embarrassed to contact them. They would surely want to know why she was no longer attending school there.

One day, while walking about in her neighborhood, Faith ran into one of her childhood friends named Dwedor. She and Dwedor had attended elementary school together in Cavalla. To her surprise, Dwedor lived only ten minutes away from her. She was very happy that they could resume their friendship. Dwedor's mother also remembered Faith as a child when she lived in Cavalla. She and Dwedor became close friends and visited each other often. But she preferred visiting Dwedor more because she was always invited to share meals with her friend and her mother. Dwedor's mother could afford to buy more food and other necessities, and understanding their plight, she didn't mind sharing what she had with them. Once again, she found herself relying on the goodness of a friend and her mother.

As Faith and Dwedor's friendship grew, she began to feel happy again. They both attended a neighborhood public school where it was easy to walk to and from school. However, it wasn't long before Faith realized that even though Dwedor's situation was much better than hers, her family was also experiencing some financial difficulties. Dwedor's mother could not afford to buy all her books and school supplies, but Faith's situation was worse. Many of the friends she met through Dwedor were taking care of themselves with very little help from their parents. Most of the families in her new neighborhood were of single-parent households facing financial difficulties.

One day, as Faith and Dwedor were walking down the street from Dwedor's house, Dwedor suddenly said to Faith, "Say thanks to that man who's passing by over there."

Faith looked in the direction Dwedor suggested, across the street from them. Her eyes met the eyes of a man she did not know. Embarrassed, she quickly looked away.

"Why should I thank him? I don't know him." Faith was clearly confused.

"Just do as I say, I will explain later," Dwedor insisted.

"Okay, I will," Faith said and thanked the man.

"You're welcome," the man, Mr. Sedeke replied.

When he turned the corner and was out of sight, Dwedor disclosed the truth about why she had asked Faith to thank a man she did not know.

She said, "You see, that man told me that he is in love with you."

"And so?" Faith retorted.

"Well," Dwedor hesitated for a minute.

"Well what?" Faith insisted.

"I told him that you needed some money, and he gave it to me."

"How could you do such a thing? Why did you tell such a lie, Dwedor?"

"I'm sorry, Faith, I needed the money so badly, and I knew he would give me the money if I said you needed it."

"Don't you ever do such a thing again, never, ever again!"

Faith tried hard to hold back the tears welling up in her eyes. She was furious because at an early age, she was taught not to engage in telling lies or any falsehood. It hurt her that her friend had engaged in lying and begging a stranger for money.

"I'm sorry, Faith, and I will never do it again. Please forgive me," Dwedor pleaded.

"Okay, Dwedor," Faith relented.

"Are we still friends, Faith?" Dwedor asked.

"We are friends forever but please do not do it again," Faith cautioned.

"Thanks, Faith," Dwedor responded, feeling relieved.

After that incident, Faith avoided going to Dwedor's neighborhood for fear of running into Mr. Sedeke. She learned that some men were allegedly poisoning women whom they had given money to but refused to succumb to their wishes. This made Faith worried and upset that Dwedor accepted Mr. Sedeke's money on her behalf, even though she had no prior knowledge of the arrangement. Dwedor began visiting her more and bringing her food whenever she could. Faith felt sad about the situation that she, as well as many young girls, found themselves in due to poverty. They were left to their own devises to fend for themselves, and many of them did almost anything to survive. This was the kind of lifestyle that Faith's upbringing with Mama and Dada did not prepare her for. And she did not know how she would support herself when her mother was still struggling to find a way to provide for her and her siblings. She could not imagine submitting to men for money what seemed to be an acceptable way of life. It was so demoralizing and abusive. She was faced with a predicament. Would she have to join the bandwagon to support herself? Did her mother expect her to engage in such despicable way of life to survive? What would be Dada and Mama's advice to her concerning this matter? She recalled Mama's last words of advice to her. How would she live by her advice when she was so defenseless? She cried because she did not know what to do.

Night School

Faith continued to attend the public school, now a ninth grader. However, she felt the pressure of her stresses mounting as she struggled to keep her head aboveboard. The only uniform she had was badly faded, and other financial demands were about to break her determination to stay aboveboard. Overwhelmed and frustrated with her situation, she decided to drop out of school. Dwedor knew Faith was a very good student when they were at Cavalla Elementary School. So she encouraged her to continue her education by going to night school, where uniforms and textbooks were not required.

Transferring to night school wasn't what Faith wanted to do, but she knew that was the only option she had to continue her education. So she was grateful that Dwedor had enlightened her to night school. It would be better than dropping out of school all together. Dwedor assisted her by asking a friend who taught at Caine Night School to help her through the enrollment process. Upon enrolling, she was amazed to find out that most of the students at the school were older men and women who had families with children. Nonetheless, she wasn't discouraged by that; she was grateful for the opportunity to continue her education. Some of her former classmates were shocked to learn that she was attending night school and wanted to know why. They told her that she did not belong in night school because she was a young lady, that she belonged in day school with her peers. She listened but was embarrassed to tell them that she didn't have the money for uniforms, textbooks, and other school supplies that day school required.

One evening, while she was on her way to school, she met some old friends from a neighborhood where she had first lived with her mother. They invited her to attend a party at a popular entertainment location where young people usually socialized called Coconut Plantation Bowling Center. At the party, Faith noticed a handsome young man, who many of the girls seemed to be attracted to. But she did not pay much attention to him because she thought with all the attention he was already receiving, he would not be looking her way. She also considered that with all the difficulties she was experiencing, there was no room in her life for more complications. In addition, she was embarrassed about her living situation, sharing a single room with her mother and siblings. She would never be able to invite anyone to meet her family.

Faith and Henry

To Faith's surprise, the handsome man noticed her, extricated himself from the flock of girls around him, and walked over to her. He simply introduced himself to her as Henry, and she reciprocated by telling him her name. It was a good feeling to know that he was attracted to her. And she also felt attracted to him but appeared rather shy. Her shyness soon melted away when Henry began to talk to her as they sat on a bench in the bowling center.

"You're so beautiful," he began, looking directly into her eyes.

"Thank you." She blushed and turned her face away from him.

"Hey! Don't be shy. Let your beauty shine."

"Stop it, Henry, you're embarrassing me with all this talk about beauty."

"Can I ask a question, Faith?"

"About what?"

"Ahh…" he stuttered as if a stuttering spell had suddenly come over him. But he was not a stutterer, a fact established since they began talking about thirty minutes prior.

"Talk about me being shy, who's being shy now?" She teased him.

"No, no, no, I'm not being shy." Henry defended himself, feeling embarrassed. "I'm making sure I gathered my thoughts before I make a fool of myself."

"Okay, Mr. Thoughtful." She teased him again. They laughed.

"Okay, let me ask for real now. I want to ask you if I could see you again because I enjoy your company."

"See me again? Where are you going to meet me because I do not have a big home?"

"If I come for you after night school, could I continue to see you?"

"Oh yeah? Would you not see me then if you did not pick me up from school?"

"Stop being so technical, Ms. Attorney-at-Law, and get serious."

"I am!" She slapped him playfully on his hand.

"So what's your response?"

"Let me think about it, and I will let you know in two days."

"In two days, right?"

"Right. I live on Carey Street in the back of Harris School."

"Isn't that something?"

"What, Henry?"

"My uncle lives on Carey Street too, just a block away."

"Small world, small world," Faith responded.

They stood up, hugged each other, and said goodbye. Immediately afterward, her friend who had invited her to the party called out to her.

"Come on, Faith, it's time to go home!"

Two days later, Henry met Faith on Carey Street where she had given him permission to visit her whenever he visited his uncle, but he wanted to see her more often. So he asked her if she could accompany him for dinner at his uncle's home on weekdays. She was only too happy to accept his offer. At least on those days, she would have nutritious meals. But during the weekends, he did not visit his uncle, so she had to fend for herself. He tried to save money for the weekdays. Henry wanted to see Faith all week, but he was not earning that much money to spend on transportation on the weekends. It was hard on both of them because they were inseparable. Henry had a burning desire to see her every day. He picked Faith up every evening after school, and they had dinner at his uncle's home during the week. His uncle's cook liked having Faith for dinner, and so she was always included in the meals.

Henry and Faith were young, deeply in love, and inseparable. He was diligent in picking her up from school each night and eventually became solely responsible for her well-being. Although his job did not pay much, he practically provided all her needs. He wanted to do more for her. And of course, he wanted to reap the benefits of his kindness. So one day at dinner, he decided to explore taking their relationship to the next level.

He began by saying, "Faith, can I ask you something?"

"Sure, Mr. Question Box."

"Are you comfortable sleeping in that small room with your mother and siblings?"

"No, I am not, but there is no other option, so I have to endure."

"You do not have to endure, unless you want to because I have an option for you."

"What option do you have, Henry?" Faith asked with a smile.

"Ahh…can you move in with me? It is just me in my room, and it is bigger. I can share it with you, and you will not have all the problems you are having now living with your mother. I have a refrigerator with lots of food. You can prepare what you want to eat and sleep in a comfortable bed."

As she listened to him trying to convince her about moving in with him, she thought about how wonderful it would be not to have to sleep crammed in a small room with her mother and two siblings, as well as all their belongings. Sleeping every night was uncomfortable and stuffy to say the least.

Without much hesitation, Faith graciously accepted Henry's suggestion and moved in with him shortly afterward. Her mother did not mind her decision to live with Henry, and she asked no questions. She was experiencing severe hardship and could barely provide for Faith and her other children. And so with Faith leaving, it meant that she had one less child to worry about. Faith was also relieved that she would be living in a place that was more spacious. And as Henry had pointed out, she didn't have the worry about not having food to eat daily. Just the thought of not having to worry about food was a significant stress reliever. She was definitely happy to be living with Henry, and he was equally happy with the way things turned out. The girl he was madly in love with was now sleeping next to him in his bed in his room. What more could he ask for? His friends even commented on a certain glow and swagger to his walk that he seemed to have suddenly acquired. Henry was so delighted to have Faith fully in his life that he could not wait to share his joy with his family members who lived in a distant rural city.

So shortly after she moved in with him, he took her on a long trip more than a hundred miles away to the rural city of Gbarnga to meet his family. He was anxious to have them meet the girl he had fallen head over heels in love with. And Faith was nervous because she wasn't sure they would like her. However, when they arrived at his parents' home, she was welcomed with opened arms by everyone. They fell in love with her from the onset. There were eleven members of Henry's family, and they treated her as one of them. She and his oldest sister bonded well and had easy conversations. Both Henry and Faith were so pleased with his family's acceptance of her that they didn't mind the long trips some weekends to visit. They had so much fun together, so it was always good to spend time with them. And Faith grew to love and consider them her other family.

Henry and Faith lived together like husband and wife. And even though he was the sole breadwinner, she believed they were mutually taking care of each other's needs. He took care of her security needs and she, his emotional needs. So after sharing a bed for about a year, she got pregnant. However, she was not happy at all about her pregnancy. It bothered her that she had not followed Mama's final words of wisdom and advice to her about boys, pregnancy, and marriage.

"Oh, Henry, I am pregnant," she cried. "I really was not expecting to get pregnant before marriage. Mama advised me to get married before having a baby. Now I'm pregnant out of wedlock. What shall we do?"

"Oh, Faith, don't you worry about it. It has happened, so we must do the best we can. I am excited to have a baby." He assured her.

He gently rubbed her abdomen hoping to feel the baby's presence. But it was too early to feel any movement or see a difference of her abdomen.

"She warned me, and I did the very thing that she warned me not to do. What a shame."

"Don't you worry and beat yourself up like that, baby. We will make everything all right because we will get married."

He sat on the bed beside her and wrapped his arms around her. Resting her head on his shoulder, he rocked back and forth as one would an upset child.

"Now listen to me, Faith, and trust me on this. I promise we will get married as soon as we can afford to have a wedding."

"Henry, it would be disgraceful if I do not have a reception and an apartment to take our baby to. It is no longer just you and me. Another life will be added to us, our baby…"

"When I get a better job and save some money, it will be possible to do all those things."

As she considered the reality of having a baby before marriage and marriage before financial stability, she began to feel very nauseated.

To avoid further discussion and aggravation, she said, "Okay, Henry, I love you and I trust you."

During the following months, Faith had a difficult time with morning sickness, nausea, and vomiting. She felt miserable and needed to see a doctor, but Henry did not have the money to send her to a private hospital to see an obstetrician. And so he decided to ask his uncle Robert, who lived and worked in Yekepa, for help. Yekepa was a small city in Northeastern Liberia, which was home to a European iron ore mining company called LAMCO. This company was largely responsible for the development of this city for its expatriate and local workers. They built a modern city comprised of residential areas, schools, shopping centers, and a well-equipped hospital to meet the needs of its employees and their families. So since Henry's uncle Robert worked for LAMCO and had access to the hospital as an employee, his mother advised him to take Faith to Yekepa to receive the necessary prenatal care she badly needed. Uncle

Robert was willing to help his nephew's pregnant fiancée get the care that was crucial for her and her unborn child. Furthermore, he and his wife agreed to have Faith live with them during the remaining months of her pregnancy.

Yekepa was more than two hundred miles away from Monrovia, where she and Henry lived. She knew it was going to be difficult being away from Henry; she would miss him too much. But on the other hand, she knew how important it was for her to get prenatal care. And there was no place better than the hospital in Yekepa to receive it. So with heavy hearts, they departed Monrovia for Yekepa where he would leave her to live temporarily with his uncle and his family. He had mixed feelings about leaving her, but this was the best decision for her and their unborn child to have the best medical care available. Yet he was sad returning to Monrovia without her, to keep his job. However, he diligently made the long journey to see her as often as he could, bringing her favorite goodies.

As a member of the family, Uncle Robert was able to have Faith registered at Yekepa Hospital where she immediately began to receive prenatal care. After a few months, Faith had a beautiful baby girl, whom she named Holly. Henry received the news about the birth of his first child. Feeling overjoyed, he rushed to Yekepa to see his beloved Faith and baby daughter. It was an exciting time for both of them. Thanking her for giving him a child, he showered her with gifts of her favorite chocolates, new clothes, and loads of food items for her and the newborn. He couldn't get enough of cuddling and adoring their child. However, after a week with Faith and Holly, he reluctantly had to return to Monrovia for work. They could not accompany him just yet because the baby was still in need of neonatal care. In addition, it was too early after the baby's birth for them to make the tedious journey back to Monrovia. On Henry's next visit, Faith did not want him to leave her and Holly again. She needed him by her side. But he was not yet ready to take them back to Monrovia, explaining that he was in search of a better job to afford a bigger apartment for them. He encouraged her to be patient and understanding and to know that he wanted them with him, but that he needed a little more time before he could take them home. Faith was so sad to see him leave, but she knew he wanted the best for her and the baby. And she believed he was working hard to achieve that.

After several visits to see Faith and his baby daughter, Holly, Henry finally had good news for them. A shipping company was hiring him with a wage much higher than that of his current job. He told her he was very excited that he would be earning more money; he would be able to make them happy. He assured her that with a higher monthly income, he would be able to provide better quality of life for them. Even though Faith liked the idea of Henry earning a higher income, she wasn't excited about him leaving her and Holly to work for a shipping company at sea. She dreaded that the job would keep them apart for much longer periods. He tried to console her that the separation would not be forever, but she had misgivings and couldn't stop herself from crying on and off during the night before his departure. The next day was a sad one for them. When he was about to leave, he kissed Faith and his baby daughter, embracing them tightly and saying words of encouragement. Faith gave him her blessing while fighting back the tears. They continued to hold onto each other with the baby between them, not wanting to let go. Finally, after a long moment, they parted. Reluctantly, he left, promising to write often and visit whenever his ship returned to the port of Monrovia.

As soon as Henry was gone, Faith immediately felt a surge of loneliness, even though she was not completely alone. She still had Holly and Henry's uncle and aunt's assurance that she and her baby would continue to be welcomed in their home. They were good to her and her child. And she was ever so grateful to them, acknowledging that she wouldn't have made it from day to day without their help. However, without any of her family members or friends around and Henry off at sea, she was overwhelmed with sadness. She became depressed and felt like she was losing her mind. Suddenly, she felt the urge to be back to what was familiar to her, Monrovia, where her mother, her siblings, and her friends were.

Back in Monrovia

In her desperation to maintain her sanity, Faith decided to move back to Monrovia, where all her friends and family lived. Somehow, she realized that depression was getting the best of her, and she was afraid that she would end up in a hospital with no one to take care of her baby. She knew she would find some support in Monrovia, even though she had no home there. However, Uncle Robert decided to take her and the baby to his sister, Ma Victoria, Henry's mother, who lived in Gbarnga, more than a hundred miles away from Monrovia. Ma Victoria was happy to see Faith and her newborn granddaughter and didn't mind them spending time with her. However, Faith was disappointed that there was no one close to her age at Ma Victoria's home at the time. All of Henry's siblings were away at boarding school. And even though Ma Victoria was good to her and her grandchild, she continued to feel sad. She thought more and more about going back to Monrovia; this would alleviate her depression and loneliness. So after a week with Ma Victoria, Faith moved to Monrovia with very little money to sustain her baby and herself. To add to her frustration, she had not heard from Henry for some time, and she was anxious for any news from him, which would greatly uplift her spirits.

During the long journey from Gbarnga to Monrovia, Faith spent most of the time pondering over where she and Holly would live. She knew her mother could not accommodate them as her financial situation had not improved since she left her to live with Henry over two years ago. The only option she thought she had was Ma Velma's home. Ma Velma was very kind to her mother and her children when they rented a room in her home a few years ago. She knew that Ma Velma would be very understanding of her plight and be willing to help her. So when Faith arrived at Ma Velma's doorsteps, the entire family ran out to welcome her and Holly.

"Oh, she's so cute. When did you have the baby, Faith?" Ma Velma asked excitedly as she took Holly from her, admiring the baby girl.

"Four months ago," Faith answered proudly.

"But where is the baby's father?" Ma Velma asked.

"He went to work on a ship overseas," Faith answered guardedly.

"Okay, overseas, eh?" Ma Velma prompted for more information.

"Yes, ma'am," Faith answered, reluctant to say more.

"Well, we are happy to see you and your cute little baby," Ma Velma said, changing the subject. She realized Faith was not ready to tell her more. She hoped that in time, she would be more opened about her situation.

"Come in, Faith, and join us for dinner. We were just getting ready to eat," Ma Velma said, handing the baby back to Faith.

They all walked into the dining room and sat down around the dining table. A plate was added to the table for Faith. She was so grateful for Ma Velma's understanding and kindness. She knew she would be welcomed in her home. Faith enjoyed the dinner of rice and beans. Being very hungry from the long journey, she ate well while thanking Ma Velma and her family for their kindness.

Although Faith had not sent a written or verbal message to Ma Velma, asking to live with her until she found a place of her own, Ma Velma sensed that she came to her because she had nowhere else to go with her baby. Her home was crowded, but she and her family made adjustment to accommodate Faith and her baby. Faith told them how much she appreciated their sacrifice and hospitality. She sensed, however, that Ma Velma and her family were embarrassed to ask her to leave, knowing that she had no means to afford a place of her own.

She also felt guilty that she had appeared at their home without prior notice to them. Even though she knew she was infringing and taking advantage of their kindness, her situation was desperate. She was anxiously awaiting to hear from Henry and hoping to receive some money from him to rent a room for Holly and herself.

One day, Ma Velma's husband, Mr. Johnson, who had worked with Faith's Uncle Ben Lewis for some time, decided it was time to let him know that his niece and her baby were outliving their welcome in his home. Uncle Ben was one of Mr. Johnson's senior staff member where they worked. So Mr. Johnson struck a conversation with him.

"How are you doing this morning, sir?" he asked Mr. Lewis.

"Fine, sir, thanks for asking." Uncle Ben was wondering what this unusual greeting was about because Mr. Johnson seldom stopped and held a conversation with him like this. He always greeted on the run.

"Do you know that your niece, Faith, is staying at my house? Matter of fact, she and her baby have been living with us for about a week now."

"I did not know where she was. Last time I heard, she was pregnant, and she had moved to Yekepa…" Mr. Lewis responded.

"Well, now you know her whereabouts. She has the cutest of babies, and she and that baby are in my home this very minute."

Mr. Johnson glanced at the wristwatch to drive home his point.

"Thanks, Mr. Johnson, for the information," Mr. Lewis said.

"There is still more, sir, Faith is having problems. She has a baby but have no food or place for them to live. My house is crowded, and you know, sir, I have many children. I really feel sorry for Faith, but I cannot continue to help her, sir. I wish I could, but I can't." Mr. Johnson paused for Mr. Lewis' response.

"Okay, Mr. Johnson, thanks so much for keeping her. I will pick her up tomorrow so that she and her baby can live with my family. I am so very sorry for the inconvenience." He sounded apologetic.

"You are welcome, sir, I thank you for responding so positively because Faith's situation is very pitiful," Mr. Johnson added.

"No, don't thank me. I should thank you. I owe you much gratitude for what you and your family have done for my niece," Mr. Lewis responded.

With mixed feelings of guilt and pride, Faith's Uncle Ben drove to Ma Velma's home the next day to get his niece and her baby. Faith packed her few belongings, thanked Ma Velma and her family, and said goodbye. She did not know how her uncle Ben knew where she was until later. She didn't go to Uncle Ben's house in the first place because she feared they wouldn't take her in, recalling the poor reception she received from them the last time they were in contact.

Faith and her baby moved in with Uncle Ben and his family. It was also crowded, but there was more room than at Ma Velma's home. Uncle Ben's family was also financially more stable. However, Faith could see the dissatisfaction on some of the family members' faces, and she sometimes overheard them making negative comments. She did not get angry because she understood their frustration with her being in their space. She quietly bore the embarrassment because she and her baby had a place to sleep and food to eat every day. Besides, she did whatever she could to please everyone as she was afraid to end up on the streets with her baby.

House of Faith Church

The House of Faith was a popular place for worship. Faith was passing in a car one day and saw people going into church not very far from where she lived. She decided that one day, she would go there, and so after two days, she went there. She enjoyed the service so much that she decided that she would be a regular member there. Faith was going through a lot of problems at the time, and every time she attended church services, she felt a sense of relief. It was like a burden was lifted. This was a different type of service from what she experienced in the Episcopal Church. There was loud singing and dancing at the House of Faith Church, and everyone seemed to be in a good mood. So she attended services at House of Faith Church whenever it was possible. She became almost addicted to the church because positive energy electrified the sanctuary.

On Sundays, she took her baby to church because services were held during the day. On Wednesdays and Fridays, services were held in the evening. For her to go to evening services without her baby, she had to do all her chores, plus the chores of some members of the family, in exchange for babysitting. When she started learning how to pray at church, she discovered that talking to the Creator was a healing balm. It gave her a surge of calmness, relaxed her tense body, and reduced her depression and loneliness. She did not want to miss any service because it was totally healing.

One afternoon, while running an errand in the heart of the city, Faith met one of Henry's friends, Orlando, who worked on the same ship with Henry. Orlando told her that he had been searching for her because Henry had sent a message by him for her. Henry wanted to send some money to her but did not know exactly where to send it. She was so happy to finally hear from Henry, especially that he wanted to send her some money, which she badly needed. So she told Orlando to let Henry know to send the money in care of a relative named, Ann Jemima. She quickly gave him her address, indicating that it would be the safest place to send it. This chance meeting on the street with Orlando was the best thing that had happened to her in a long time.

Within a few weeks, Ann Jemima informed Faith that she had received a letter from Henry for her. So excited, she rushed to pick up her letter and immediately burst into tears of joy when she opened it and saw a note and money from Henry. She was overcome with a mix of joy and sadness. On one hand, she was very happy for the much-needed money, but on the other, feeling sad about missing her beloved Henry, the father of her child. Most of the money he sent was used to buy food for her baby and personal items that she badly needed. She also bought herself a new pair of flip-flop slippers to replace the one pair that was totally worn out. In the letter he wrote, he promised to send more money the next time, and thereafter, a fixed amount monthly.

"Oh, how wonderful that would be. A monthly allowance would allow me to rent a room for Holly and me," she said to herself.

She couldn't wait to stop depending on others for her livelihood; she needed a place of her own.

It wasn't long before Faith would once again find herself and her baby daughter without a home. Unexpectedly, one afternoon, Uncle Ben's oldest daughter, Hannah, who lived in the city, came to visit her parents. Shortly after her arrival at her parents' home, she engaged Faith in a one-on-one conversation on the porch.

"Faith, some members of my family do not want you and your baby living with them in this house anymore." She began.

"I do not believe you, Hannah, because I do everything to please everyone around here," Faith said angrily.

"Let me tell you, honey, like it really is. Your uncle Ben is embarrassed to tell you to leave, and there is a lot of quarrel in this house about you living here." Hannah pointed out.

"What!" Faith exclaimed.

"Shocking, eh?" Hannah said.

"But where am I going to go with my baby?" Faith said tearfully.

"I have no clue, honey, but I know they do not want you and your baby in this house any longer," Hannah added carelessly.

"I will move, Hannah, there is no need to stay if I am not wanted here," Faith replied, wearily.

"I'm sorry, honey, I wish I could help you and that cute baby of yours, but I really can't," Hannah retorted.

"Thanks, Hannah, for telling me," Faith responded, clearly upset.

She hurried away from the porch into the living room where Uncle Ben sat smoking a cigarette.

"What's the matter, Faith?" Uncle Ben asked.

"What's the matter? Why didn't you just tell me to my face instead of talking behind my back?" Faith asked angrily.

"Talking about what behind your back?" Uncle Ben prompted, pretending to be oblivious about what she was talking about.

"Uncle Ben, you know very well what I am talking about," Faith snapped. "You do not want me in your house. Thanks for accommodating me and my daughter for the time we have been here. Since we have been such an unbearable inconvenience for you and your family, we are leaving today!" Faith pointed out, clearly frustrated.

"Where are you going to go?" Uncle Ben asked.

"I do not know, but God will make a way for me." She cried.

"Well, here is ten-dollars for your transportation." He pulled a ten-dollar bill out of his wallet and gave it to her.

"Thanks, Uncle Ben, and goodbye to you and your family."

She took the money from her uncle's hand and stormed out of the living room. She then went into her room, gathered her few belongings, took her baby, and stormed out of Uncle Ben's house.

In a hurried decision, she took a taxi to her friend's Clara house in another part of town. Clara did not have enough space in her home, but she felt sorry about her friend's predicament and agreed to let her and her daughter stay temporarily with her.

In frustration and embarrassment, the thought of returning to her baby's grandmother, Ma Victoria's home in Gbarnga, briefly crossed her mind, but she quickly abandoned the idea. She was afraid moving back would bring back feelings of loneliness and depression. She remembered how she felt close to losing her mind. She couldn't bear the thought of living in isolation of her friends and family. And the fact that telephone service in rural parts, where Ma Victoria lived, was almost nonexistent. She was unable to keep in touch with the people she cherished in her life. All these things added to her misery while she lived there, and she dared not move back. However, the most profound thing about living with Ma Victoria was the constant reminder of Henry's absence. In a way, it was embarrassing that he wasn't keeping in touch with his mother and very seldom with her. And so for her emotional and spiritual well-being, Faith decided that Monrovia was where she needed to be. At least in Monrovia, she sometimes had fun with friends and, most importantly, attended House of Faith Church where she found succor for her tortured soul.

Chapter 9

Working for House of Faith Church

Temporarily, Faith was living with Clara, but she needed a place to live that could give her a sense of permanence and security. Therefore, she went to House of Faith and confided in Pastor Bendu, explaining that she and her daughter were teetering on the brink of homelessness. The pastor told her that she could hire her as a receptionist for the church and provide her with food, but she could not bring her child to work. So Faith had to find someone to take care of her baby while she worked, and she could not live in the church's shelter because the shelter only accommodated young women without children. Feeling helpless and needy, she had no choice but to accept the terms of Pastor Bendu's offer. Nevertheless, she was faced with the challenge of finding someone to take care of her baby. In fact, Pastor Bendu even asked a few members of the church if they could help her with the baby, but no one offered to help.

Since she was so badly in need of a job, Faith asked Pastor Bendu to give her a week to find someone to take care of her baby before starting work. The pastor agreed. So Faith decided to seek the help of her biological sister, Miatta, whom she had moved in with after leaving her friend's Clara's home. She pleaded with her sister and suggested a deal that would benefit both of them—that Miatta take care of her own daughter and Holly during the day while Faith was at work. And in turn, she would take care of Holly and Miatta's daughter at night while Miatta was at work. But Miatta rejected the suggestion and argued that she could not take care of two children during the day because she needed time to sleep. Faith clearly understood Miatta's position, but she still had the challenge of finding care for Holly.

In desperation, Faith decided to take Holly back to her grandmother, Ma Victoria, who lived over a hundred miles away in Gbarnga. Ma Victoria agreed to care for her grandchild. Even though she had short notice, she was in empathy with Faith's situation. After all, her son, Henry, was working overseas to make life better for them. And so she was willing to help. Faith thank Ma Victoria for coming to her rescue with Holly. She was torn and heartbroken leaving her daughter, but she needed to earn money to support both of them. And so she hugged and kissed her baby, said goodbye and returned to Monrovia and living with her sister, Miatta, in a small room. The agreement between the two sisters was that Faith would move out into her own room when she saved enough money from her new job. Faith finally began her new job as a receptionist for House of Faith Church shortly after her return from Ma Victoria. Her salary was $25.00 a month, including a free meal each day. Faith was grateful for the job.

Although Faith was grateful for the steady income, she had misgivings about Holly being so far away from her. She was happy for the employment but sad because her baby now lived three hours away in Gbarnga, and she could not see her daily. To rest easier, she encouraged herself that the separation from her daughter was only temporary, that as soon as she had saved enough money to rent a room, she would get Holly back from her grandmother.

Since Faith lived five miles away from House of Faith Church, she commuted to work by city bus each weekday. Her weekly bus fares totaled $2.00 dollars a week. By the end of the month, the bus fare had taken away $8.00 of the $25.00 dollars a month salary she earned. She had to give her sister little change sometimes. The possibility of saving enough money to get a room for herself and her baby

42

seemed very grim because she had to buy food and other essentials with the remaining money. On the weekends, she had to buy her own food to prepare because she was off from work.

Because of the continuing hardship Faith was enduring, she often slipped into deep thoughts as she rode on the public bus going to and from work.

"I wish Henry could come soon to take care of the baby and me. Hard times do not seem to end, not even with a job. I thought things would improve but hard times continue."

Worry and impatience became Faith's daily mental diet. She worried about her daughter, Holly, her honey, Henry, and the fact that she would not be able to keep her agreement with Miatta to rent her own room as soon as possible. Regardless of her troubled mind, she remained hopeful that Henry would keep his promise to send her a monthly allowance. It would greatly enable her in getting a rental room. Since the first time he wrote and sent her some money, she had not heard from him. However, she was waiting patiently, but worry was slowly sinking in. She missed him very much and was sometimes overcome with sadness when she thought about him. Often when she slipped into depressive moods thinking about him, she found comfort in prayers. She was grateful that House of Faith taught her how to pray and look up to God for solace and deliverance. When she prayed, she was comforted. The church became her refuge for praying and prayer, her source of consolation.

After Holly had lived with her grandmother for a while, Faith went to see her. The baby seemed to be doing well. In fact, Ma Victoria had a lot of help from the neighbors with Holly. She was pleased with how well Holly's grandmother was taking care of her. However, Faith's satisfaction and gratitude for Ma Victoria's care for her daughter was short-lived because things soon changed for the worse.

A few months after Faith's visit to see her daughter, Ma Victoria sent a message to Pastor Bendu at House of Faith Church, where she worked. Upon receiving the message, Pastor Bendu called Faith into her office and told her that Ma Victoria needed to see her in Gbarnga as soon as possible. Faith was very troubled about the urgency of the message but avoided asking the pastor why Ma Victoria wanted to see her so urgently. Instead of disclosing Ma Victoria's full message to her, Pastor Bendu simply told her that she needed to leave immediately and suggested that a member of the church accompany her. Faith was grateful for the company of Sister Eva, a prominent member of the church, on the journey to Gbarnga. And she was also thankful to Pastor Bendu for paying all the travel expenses. Everything seemed so suspicious. And Faith had a weird feeling that something was not right but did not know exactly what.

The three-hour journey to Gbarnga seemed to take forever. As Faith sat quietly lost in thoughts, her anxiety continued to rise. She kept reminding herself to remain calm and keep hopeful that everything was fine, but it seemed impossible. As soon as she and Sister Eva arrived at Ma Victoria's home and saw everyone crying but didn't see Holly, her greatest fear was realized. She learned that her beautiful baby girl, Holly, was dead. The reality of Holly's death shocked Faith so much that she could not cry. Overcome with shock and anguish, she felt an excruciating pain in the depth of her soul at such an unimaginable loss. Ma Victoria, trying to console her, wrapped her arms around Faith, cried and begged for forgiveness. She told Faith that Holly had developed a very high fever, and so she took her to see the nurse, who treated everyone in town. The nurse diagnosed her with high fever due of malaria. He gave Holly medication, but she never recovered. There were no hospitals nearby, so only the nurses were available to help around.

If Faith had not learned how to pray, she would have lost her mind and ended up in a mental institution. Fervent prayers sustained and kept her anchored in her faith in God, but yet, she felt alone in her grief with no family member by her side. So after Holly's burial, she returned to Monrovia the next day and went back to work brokenhearted, sad and lonely. She was still living with her sister and was grateful to her. She felt extremely indebted to her.

Several months after Holly's tragic death, Faith continued to lament, trying to rationalize how something so dreadful could happen to her beautiful baby girl. She believed Ma Victoria, Henry's mother, was a good woman, who cared dearly for her granddaughter.

Sometimes there are bad things that happen to good people. She did not know things would end up like this. In fairness, however, there was no reliable way to communicate across the miles. Only a few workers owned telephones, which, in most cases, were unusable due to connection problems. And Ma Victoria did not own one; neither did Faith. Messages and news were transferred from place to place mostly by the movement of people from place to place. Faith knew that it was time to let Henry know about the death of their child. She had remained silent for too long because she did not know how to break the dreadful news to him, but she knew she had to let him know soon. Therefore, she had to find Orlando. As far as she knew, he was the only reliable means by which to send a message to Henry.

And so with heavy heart, she wrote a letter to Henry to inform him about their daughter's death. At that time, Henry's coworker, Orlando, was awaiting an assignment in Monrovia to return to work on the ship. He was the only hope for her getting a message to Henry. And so she was relieved when Orlando finally received another assignment and went back to work on the ship. Once he was onboard the ship, Orlando wasted no time finding Henry and giving him the letter from Faith, knowing the gravity of the message enclosed. Henry's reply to Faith's letter was a very solemn one. He indicated how shocking and devastating the news of Holly's death was and how much he cried. And then he concluded by saying that he did not think he could return to Monrovia. Faith wasn't expecting to hear this from Henry at all, and it frightened and worried her. She couldn't imagine that Henry really meant what she understood from his letter, that their relationship was over. However, regardless of the implication of his letter, she continued to wait and didn't lose hope that he would come back to Monrovia to see and comfort her. She was still very much in love with him and did not find herself attracted to any other man.

As time went by, Faith became more active in her church. She began singing and became the lead soloist. In addition, she worked long hours daily and stayed after work twice a week for church services, as well as attending service every Sunday morning. Faith's salary increased to $30.00 a month. A portion of her meager income was used to buy white uniforms to wear to work and services. She wished she could find a job that paid more money as her monthly expenses were not being met, but she knew that it would be difficult for her finding such a job since she had not completed high school. Without a high school diploma, her chances of finding a job that paid more were slim. And although the idea of returning to night school was always on her mind, she knew that she could not afford the added expenses for school. She would need money for public transportation to and from school as well as to buy school supplies.

Reliving the Past

Two years after Holly's death, Faith found herself unmarried and pregnant again while working at House of Faith Church. The reality of her second pregnancy flooded her mind with bitter memories. She recalled Henry's separation from her during her first pregnancy, how she and their child struggled to survive, the loneliness and sadness she felt when Holly died tragically, and Henry's devastating decision to never return home. Circumstances surrounding her second pregnancy were no better than the first. She did not know what to do, but she knew an abortion was not an option. She tried to hide the pregnancy, but morning sickness associated with pregnancy betrayed her efforts. Experienced women in the church could see the telltale signs.

Because it was becoming apparent that she couldn't continue to pretend any longer, Faith decided to confess her pregnancy. And so she confided in Mary, a woman five years her senior, who was also a member of the church. She pleaded with Mary to keep the information confidential, but Mary told Pastor Bendu anyway. The pastor then had a meeting with Faith alone.

"Words have reached my ears that you are pregnant…"

"Who told you so, Pastor?" Faith interrupted.

"Never mind who told me. All I want to know is, is the rumor true or false?"

"Why don't people just mind their own business…"

"Listen, Faith, I am not talking about people here. I want to know the truth. Are you pregnant?"

"I'm so sorry, Pastor. I did not mean to get pregnant. I made a mistake." Faith sobbed.

"Never mind all that crying. Are you going to get married? You need to be truthful. You know the rules of the church."

"I am scared, Pastor, I don't want to be put out of the church." Faith sobbed bitterly.

"You knew better not to play with men because they will get you pregnant. No doubt, you still remember what you went through with your daughter. I will call a meeting with the trustees. After that meeting, I will have a talk with the man who impregnated you."

"Pastor, please do not take the job from me. I have no other means…"

"You should had thought about that before sleeping with the man."

"Please, Pastor, help me."

"There is only one thing that can keep you on the job, and it is to get married to Tom, the man who is responsible for your pregnancy."

"Married! I don't like Tom that much!"

"You and Tom must get married."

"No, please, Pastor, no." Faith sobbed.

"Listen to me, Faith, I do not want you to throw your life away, so you must get married."

"Okay, Pastor." Faith wiped away the tears from her eyes with the back of her hand.

"When you and Tom get married, I will send both of you to America to get your education. The church will sponsor you. After your studies, you will return to Liberia to work for House of Faith Church. I cannot send you if you are not married because the board of trustees will be against it. You know our policy, no having children out of wedlock. When you had your daughter, you were not a member of the church at the time, so we accepted you. I'm really trying to help you, but there is no way around our church's policy. If you and Tom do not want to get married, then I will let the church policy take its course. And you know what that will mean?"

"I will be without a job at the church, and I don't want this to happen."

"Go home and think about my suggestion. I will talk with Tom and find out what he has to say. If he refuses to marry you, you will not have a job at the church."

"I will talk with Tom too, Pastor, for us to get married so we can travel to America."

"Good! That will be all." Pastor Bendu ended the conversation.

Faith felt exhausted from her conversation with the pastor, but she knew that she had to persuade Tom to take the marriage suggestion that the pastor had offered. She had to find Tom and discuss the matter with him. She hoped he would be reasonable enough to take advantage of a relatively free education in America that she longed for.

After her meeting with Faith, Pastor Bendu met with Tom, the father-to-be of Faith's unborn baby. She literally had the same conversation with him that she had with Faith but stressing to him the risk involved, especially for Faith, if he did not take her suggestion. Faith would lose her job with the church, which was her only source of income. However, despite Tom being made aware of the predicament Faith would find herself in and the opportunity for them to further their education in the United State, he refused the pastor's offer. The fact was, neither Tom nor Faith wanted to get married. Besides that, all Faith could think about was the opportunity to go to the United States, to get out of the terrible situation and hardship she was facing. Faith was hoping that they could just go through the motions of marriage and, when they got to the United States, go their separate ways, but Tom was not interested in the idea of marriage at all. And on the other hand, Faith still loved Henry. She still had hopes that he would return home one day, and they would be happy like they were before he left to work on the ship.

After Pastor Bendu's conversation with Tom, during which he flatly refused to accept her offer of education in the United States upon marriage to Faith, the pastor was taken aback and angry at his refusal. She couldn't understand why he would refuse marriage to a beautiful young woman, who was carrying his child, as well as free education in the United States. But little did she or Faith know that Tom was living with a young woman without being married to her, and they had a son together.

Faith met Tom at House of Faith Church, where he sometimes assisted his father in construction work at the church. He owned a car and would sometimes offer people from the church ride. Faith was always happy for the free rides because that meant she didn't spend money on transportation which she could barely afford on her meager income. However, the free rides Faith thought she was getting from Tom were not free after all. She got pregnant and was left to cope alone by herself. It was no real caring relationship. So with the refusal to marry, Pastor Bendu was constraint to take the next step. She called Faith into her office and told her that she could no longer work for the church. Even though Faith had previously been advised about the consequences of the church's policy against unmarried pregnant women working for the church, being informed of her dismissal affected her like the sting of a hornet. She was so devastated that she ran into the church's prayer room to pray. Deja vu! She prayed fervently that day to the Creator.

"Lord, this is another pregnancy, and You know what I went through with the first one. I beg, please bless me with this child and let the struggles be much easier. Let this child be a blessing to me someday because I am devoted to you and have worked hard for your church. Please, Lord, bless and protect this baby and me. Amen."

"Lord God, please help me understand. I want to know how the love and mercy that House of Faith Church preaches so eloquently about justify my dismissal. Which is greater, Lord? House of Faith Church's policy or your principles of divine love and mercy?"

Faith was devastated. She had been so devoted to the church, both as an employee and a faithful member. And even though she had prior knowledge of the church's policy, she begged for forgiveness. How could they not have mercy on her? How could they fire her from her job when she had nothing?

Faith continued to live with her sister and still attended services at House of Faith Church. Most of the members she thought loved her were not concerned about her situation in the least. A few gave her some help as they could while others gossiped and spread rumors about her that made her compelled to confront them. Therefore, one day, during a testimonial service, she testified boldly and asked the worshippers a soul-searching question, "Why should I be the subject and the predicate in every conversation and gossip in this church? Please help me understand why! Why, brothers and sisters?" However, after the testimony, two prominent members of the church gave her a nickname by referring to her as "subject and predicate."

As she advanced in her pregnancy, Faith lived at the mercy of a few people who sometimes gave her food and small amounts of money. Her sister, Miatta, was struggling as well. So she could not help her beyond sharing her room with her. Faith was thankful to Miatta for a place to sleep. She believed that someday God would bring her through her storms.

A few months later, Faith went into labor. She took a cab to the hospital, and several hours later, she delivered a bouncing baby boy, weighing seven pounds and eight ounces. She named him Andrew. This was a happy time for her, which for a while overshadowed the hard times she was experiencing. Three people came to see her at the hospital. One of them was Tom, Andrew's father. He stayed ten minutes and left. The other two people were Tom's baby mother, who lived with him and her friend. They all came once, and no one else came. More surprising of all, no one from House of Faith Church, nor any of her family members came to see her and the baby.

Taxi Fare and No Home to Go To

On the day Faith was discharged from the hospital with her newborn baby, she had no one to take her home. She had only ten dollars for taxi fare to where she lived with her sister and to purchase a few things for the infant. But when she arrived at her sister's one-room residence, she found her sister gone, and the door locked. The owner of the house told Faith that her sister had moved but left no information where she had moved to. Faith was utterly speechless and terrified because she had nowhere to go with her baby. She dared not go to her mother's one congested room. And even if it were possible, she would not go back to Cousin Annabel's home. She remembered how her cousin's boyfriend had often touched her inappropriately. And even more spiteful, she remembered how she abruptly kicked her out of her home without any reasonable explanation. Her cousin's lame reason for doing so was that she had not come home immediately after her school parade even though Faith told her that she went to visit her mother.

Feeling lost and dejected, Faith walked aimlessly down the street, worried and unsure of what to do. Suddenly, it dawned on her to pause. Intuitively, she began to carefully examine names on her mental list of friends she had made over the years, including some standoffish cousins she grew up with. She was frantically searching her mind to recall the name of someone from that list who she could appeal to, to accommodate them in their home for a few days. Not readily coming up with any name, she continued walking slowly down the street with her baby. Suddenly, perhaps by divine intervention, she ran into Mydea, a friend from House of Faith Church. After greeting each other, she sadly began to explain her pitiful situation to Mydea.

"I got sick right after the delivery. And as if that wasn't enough, when I returned with my baby to my sister's room, she had moved. Nobody knows where she moved to. Here I am with a week-old baby with no home to go to."

"I'm so sorry, Faith." Mydea sobbed. Before long, both were crying on the street corner.

"Listen, Faith, don't worry. I will take you and your baby in." She took Faith and her baby to a house where she was renting two rooms for herself and her three children. She then gave Faith her children's room for she and her baby to use. Faith gratefully accepted the room but felt uneasy as the children slept on a mat on the floor. They gave up their bed to Faith and her baby.

A few days later, Faith's sister, Miatta, who had moved and left no information for her about where she had moved to, came to Mydea's house to visit her and the baby. She wove a lame story about why she did not leave her new address for her sister. Eventually, however, she told Faith that she had no room for her and her baby because her boyfriend now lived with her.

Unfortunately, Miatta's story brought back bitter memories for Faith about her struggle to find a permanent place for herself and her first child, Holly, who eventually died in that struggle. Now that horrible situation seemed to be repeating with her second child. She prayed for God's help finding a job with a higher wage to afford renting a room for her son and herself. As time went by, her prayer seemed farther away from materializing. The reality was that most young women experienced economic hardship in the city, and without a high school diploma, life was even more difficult for them. And with a newborn baby, Faith's situation was more complicated. She had no money to buy milk for the baby. Also, she didn't have enough food for herself to sustain her for breastfeeding her baby daily. Not having enough nourishment, she was feeling weak and seemed anemic but couldn't afford to see a doctor.

As Faith was praying to find a job, Mydea's landlord, Ms. Cynthia, was feeling Faith's pain. For quite some time, she watched Faith as she struggled to take care of her baby and herself and felt sorry for her. But when she could no longer just mind her own business, she had to meddle in Faith and her baby's business to literally save their lives. And so she gave Faith an unsolicited advice to take Baby Andrew to his grandfather, Tom's father, and leave him there. Ms. Cynthia knew Tom's father very well since they grew up together in the same neighborhood. She told Faith that he would be willing to help her with the baby if he knew she was struggling. Although Faith considered Ms. Cynthia's suggestion sensible and tempting, she was, however, ambivalent about it. Once again, she was reminded about her beloved Holly, who died when she took her to live with her grandmother under similar circumstances.

However, after some soul-searching and especially since she and her baby were living at the mercy of a few people who helped her with the bare necessities because they felt sorry for her and her baby, Faith decided to take Ms. Cynthia's suggestion. Feeling sad and helpless, she carried her baby to his grandfather, fearing she was making a sad mistake, but she had no choice. Without a job, she was facing dire consequences. So Faith took the child and left to look for food without the intention to come back. The baby's biological grandmother heard the story of Faith's struggles, and she decided to take care of the baby. She took the baby from the grandfather's house to live with her. She and the grandfather were divorced. That night, Faith could not sleep; she tossed and turned restlessly all night long. She was so worried about her baby and torn about whether to get him back or let him stay. So the next morning, Faith confided in Ms. Cynthia about her fear and indecisiveness. Ms. Cynthia was understanding and consoled her that her baby's grandfather earned a good salary, and she was certain he would take good care of his own grandchild. After their conversation, Faith felt much better and agreed to let Baby Andrew stay with his grandmother, but she still had a difficult time fighting the urge to retrieve her son from his grandmother. Ms. Cynthia assured her that she would realize later, that she made the right decision for her baby.

Although Baby Andrew seemed to be faring well with his grandmother, Faith continued to worry while reassuring herself that she made the right decision for him. She reasoned that with no job nor money to buy food for the baby since he could not live only on breast milk, especially when she herself had very little to eat, it was better to have him stay with his grandmother. Ms. Cynthia was afraid both she and the baby would suffer malnutrition and get sick, and during her lecture, she convinced Faith that she made the right decision.

"Faith, wisdom demands that when one cannot help oneself, one needs to seek help. Because not getting help when one needs it is foolish."

"Thanks, Ms. Cynthia, I'm just having a flashback about my first child who died under similar circumstances."

Despite the unfortunate treatment Faith received from some members of House of Faith Church, she remained a member of the church. She attended services regularly. One evening after prayer service, a friend named Comfort, also a member of the church, invited Faith to spend some time with her and her family at their home. She was excited that Comfort asked her to spend some time with them. She accepted the invitation because most of the times, she was all alone. Besides, it was embarrassing watching Mydea's children sleeping on the floor while she slept in their bed. After she took Andrew to live with his grandmother, she welcomed the children to sleep in the bed with her, but they refused. She was aware that most parents taught their children to be respectful of adults, so she understood the children's refusal to sleep in the bed with her. They felt it would be disrespectful to sleep in the bed with someone older. Moving to Comfort's home would bring relief to Mydea's children, as well as herself. The children would have their bed back, and she would stop feeling guilty about depriving them of their bed. So she packed her few belongings, thanked Mydea and her children wholeheartedly for their kindness, saying she would always be grateful for their accommodation when she and her baby were homeless.

Faith's friend, Comfort's, home was very large and elegant. With an abundance of food, the home was even more appealing to Faith. Comfort gave her a bed, which was on one side of her very spacious room. And Faith enjoyed sumptuous meals every day. She began to experience a breath of fresh air as happiness flowed into her stuffy life. Stress and weariness which hung heavily upon her body began to dissipate. As her situation improved, she decided it was time to go back to night school and complete her high school education.

Chapter 12

Trouble Once Again

Just as she was thanking God for her good fortune and getting comfortable in her new surroundings, Faith began to encounter a difficult problem at night. While everyone was fast asleep, one of Comfort's relative, named Mr. Lokko, came into the room and began to touch her in a sexual manner. She felt his hands on her while she slept and was terrified. During the day when she saw him, she was upset and afraid but did not tell Comfort about her relative's despicable nighttime behavior. She was afraid that if she told Comfort what Mr. Lokko was doing to her at night, she would be thrown out of her home since he was a family member and a strong supporter in her home. Disappointed and afraid to speak about the matter, an ingenious idea occurred to her. She borrowed a tight girdle from one of her girlfriends, Audrey. She then wore the girdle with a bra to bed the next night. When the intruder came in, he was disappointed that he could not touch her the way he wanted to. He tried several times, but the girdle and bra shielded Faith from his offensive and intrusive hands.

Nevertheless, Faith decided that it was better to find somewhere else to live because she hated and was disgusted with Mr. Lokko and his nasty ways. She did not want to create any problems in the home of a friend who was helping her. She was also aware that people were generally disinclined to talk about sexual harassment, which was problematic and rampant in society. It seemed a taboo to bring it up in any conversation. And so disclosing an act of sexual abuse was useless; nothing came out of it. In fact, young women who dared to confront or talk about sexual predators who abused them were often ridiculed and referred to as troublemakers, and they looked for the abuse.

Faith prayed every day, asking God to make a way for her out of her misery. And God responded to Faith's prayer in a dream. One night, she dreamed that she was traveling in an airplane. She did not know her destination exactly, but she remembered clearly flying on an airplane. It seemed so real that she decided to tell a friend and the secretary at House of Faith Church about it, but they dismissed it as simply a dream. However, she had a premonition that she would travel somewhere away from Liberia because the dream seemed so real.

Chapter 13

Visit to the United States

A couple of days after Faith had the dream, Pastor Bendu, who had dismissed her from her job at House of Faith Church when she got pregnant, sent her a message to come to the church. The message was the first contact from Pastor Bendu since she dismissed her from her work at the church. Even though Faith faithfully attended services after her dismissal, she always left immediately after service because the Pastor and most of the members did not want to be bothered with her. They considered her a sinner. So she was wondering why the pastor wanted to see her. However, when she met Pastor Bendu, she received the surprise of her life. The pastor had accepted an invitation to the United States for a church convention. Pastor Bendu told Faith that the Lord laid it on her heart to take her along with some members of the church to the US for the convention. Faith would sing at some of the services. The pastor told her that if she agreed to travel with them, the church would be responsible for all expenses, including personal funds to purchase her necessities for the trip.

Faith was the youngest soloist at House of Faith Church before she was dismissed from her receptionist position. It was because she got pregnant out of wedlock, in violation of one of the church's policy, that the board of trustees could not take lightly. She stopped singing at church but attended services as a regular visitor. The news of her being invited to travel with the church shocked the church's secretary. She could not understand how Faith's dream of traveling in an airplane could come into fruition so quickly. But Faith did not doubt that her dream would come true because it seemed so real. Her American Dream was about to be realized. She gladly and gratefully accepted the invitation from the pastor, thanking her profusely.

Feeling ecstatic, Faith hurried back to her girlfriend, Comfort's house, screaming that she was going to America. She was so happy that her dream to travel to the United States would take place even before most of her friends and relatives who were doing far better economically than her. The miraculous change of her circumstances brought a certain Bible verse to her mind, Matthew 21:22 (KJV), "And all things, whatsoever, ye shall ask in prayer, believing, ye shall receive. Faith believed this was truly relevant in her case."

After a long anxious wait as preparations for travel to the United States were finalized, Faith and a group of fourteen members of House of Faith Church flew from Liberia to New York City and stayed at a beautiful hotel in Manhattan before going to South Side Chicago for the convention. For the next three nights, they held praise and prayer services at one of the conference rooms at the hotel. Faith sang during those festive services, but her shining moments came when she captivated the audience with her melodious voice, singing solos at certain intervals during services. The services were attended by several Liberians, who also paid them visits at the hotel. As word spread about Pastor Bendu's powerful prayer services and the beautiful singing, attendance grew as more and more people came to partake in the services.

House of Faith Church's delegation's next trip was to Chicago. This was where the main conference they had come to attend was being held. Some of the church members, including Faith were invited to stayed at a home on South Side, Chicago. Their host owned a restaurant that stayed open twenty-four hours a day, as well as many houses on the block. Faith and her fellow church members were given free pass to eat whatever they wanted at the restaurant any time they wanted. And so Faith ate as though she had never seen food. As a matter of fact, everyone on the trip put on a few pounds because of the abundance of good food freely available to all. Faith recalled that it was only a few months ago that she was homeless and hungry. And now she had more food than she could possibly eat. She was so happy. If only she and Baby Andrew could have the opportunity to make America their home, Faith thought, her dream would be completely realized.

Working Again for House of Faith Church

Upon her return from the trip abroad, Faith was reconciled with House of Faith Church. Pastor Bendu restored her to the receptionist position and offered her rent-free board in the church's cellar. She was very happy and relieved because she could now leave Comfort's home and be rid of Mr. Lokko and his persistent attempts to abuse her sexually. She was grateful that her sincere prayers to God to deliver her from the devil had been answered.

After she moved into the church's cellar, things were fine during the dry season. But during the rainy season, the room took on different character. Whenever it rained heavily, the cellar flooded, and her bed and clothes got soaking wet floating in the water. She and the other cellar dwellers had to bail out the rainwater as it seeped in to keep it from accumulating. This was a huge exhausting exercise, extending over several months of heavy downpours during the rainy season. However, when the rainwater was too much to bail, they abandoned their cellar rooms and sought higher grounds in the church annex, where the church offices were. There were also bedrooms in the annex, but these rooms were off-limits.

Since Faith had had two children, she was not allowed to live upstairs where the pastor and the other young ladies without children lived. House of Faith Church's policy was clear and strict on that matter. It prohibited young unmarried mothers from mingling with young unmarried girls without children. Unmarried mothers were mostly ridiculed and expected not to further their education. They were expected to find men, get married, and become homemakers. Occasionally, Faith went upstairs to report to the pastor, where she would observe the young ladies at the table eating meals with the pastor. I wished that I was a part of the family, she thought. The meals upstairs seemed sumptuous and smelled delicious. However, Faith was grateful for the food she had downstairs. There were times when she had nothing to eat.

Several months after House of Faith Church's delegation returned from their conference in United States, Pastor Bendu invited Faith to travel with her to the Ivory Coast, West Africa, to attend a scheduled revival. Again, this came as a surprise to Faith, who gratefully accepted the invitation. Coincidentally, prior to Pastor Bendu inviting her to the revival in Ivory Coast, Faith had a similar dream about traveling on an airplane like she did prior to traveling to the United States. Just as she shared her first dream with the former church secretary, she also shared the second dream with Helena, the new secretary at House of Faith Church. It was not long after the second dream that Pastor Bendu invited her to travel with her to Ivory Coast.

Chapter 15

Trip to Ivory Coast

An important fact about the trip to Ivory Coast that Faith was not privy to soon came to light. Two days before the trip, the coordinator in charge of the revival planning traveled to Monrovia from the Ivory Coast with an important message from Mother Olive, the host of the impending revival, for Pastor Bendu of House of Faith Church. This was not his first time visiting the church, where he heard Faith sing on several occasions during service. The coordinator told Pastor Bendu that Mother Olive had requested Faith to accompany her to the revival. She had learned of Faith's exceptional skill as a soloist at House of Faith Church and was looking forward to her attending the revival and gracing the occasion with her angelic voice. And so she sent two plane tickets for Pastor Bendu and Faith. However, all others scheduled to attend the revival had to purchase their own plane tickets.

When the church secretary learned that Faith was going to Ivory Coast with the group, she was shocked. She jokingly pleaded with Faith not to have any bad dream about her since Faith's dreams seemed to come true every time. On the Friday before the trip, the secretary typed out a list of all those from the church scheduled to attend the revival in Ivory Coast with the pastor. Faith's name was not on the list because she had not yet received the ticket that Mother Olive was sending for Faith. The coordinator came on Saturday before the trip.

The secretary did not work on the weekend but attended service on Sunday morning.

While on her way to church that Sunday morning, the secretary bought a newspaper that had news about House of Faith Church. To her surprise, the trip to Ivory Coast was mentioned, and there was the list that she had typed with the names of all those attending. To her surprise, at the end of the list was Faith's name. She was confused because Faith's name was not included on the list that she typed. She was certain that it was an error because she knew Faith could not afford to buy a plane ticket. So when the secretary arrived at church that morning, she anxiously pointed out Faith's name in the newspaper to some of the members. They simply informed her that Faith was going because the host sent a ticket for her. Then she later learned that the pastor added Faith's name to the list on Saturday after the coordinator delivered her ticket. Saturday was the secretary's day off, so she could not have known about the change.

In a few days, the delegation from House of Faith Church, including Faith, traveled to Ivory Coast and participated in an all-inspiring praying and singing experience. Mama Olive was highly impressed by Faith's singing and complimented her. After a brief visit, the group returned to Monrovia, and Faith's confidence in the church and its members gradually began to return. Life seemed more optimistic. She hadn't felt so much at peace in a long time and was hoping that things would remain that way. For in her short life, she had experienced too many struggles and misfortune.

However, contrary to what she was hoping, she started facing problems at House of Faith Church again because of jealously. This was her second trip with the pastor, and so some members became jealous. They wanted to be the ones traveling with the pastor, so they began to tell lies to destroy her renewed relationship with the pastor, but they did not realize that she was chosen to attend those events because of her gift of singing and her diligence as a worker at the church. One example of the lies they concocted was someone told the pastor she was always talking outside in front of the church during service, instead of being in service. But what they did not understand was sometimes during the service, she sat at a desk in front of the church to record names of people who wanted to see the pastor for counseling, and that involved communicating with those people. Every day, they came up with new lies and complaints to share with the pastor. Clearly, they envied the new and improved relationship between the pastor and her. Some considered her a sinner because she had children out of wedlock although she repented and was trying to live a better life.

So Faith figured that the best thing for her to do, at that point, was to leave House of Faith Church with its deceitful members and work to improve her life by going back to school to earn her high school diploma. She reasoned that a high school diploma would qualify her for a better-paying job. It would increase her chances of finding a higher-paying job outside of the church, but she couldn't leave the church just yet because she needed a place to live and earn money while attending school.

But being determined to further her education, she enrolled and began attending classes at a community night school in the heart of the city. Some nights, when she returned home from school, the gateman at the church did not want to open the gate to let her enter the premises. He assumed that her lateness was intentional and disregarded the fact that she had to rely on public transportation. The buses were frequently very crowded in the evenings, and they did not always run on schedule. She had to wait to get on a bus that could accommodate her. Pastor Bendu also did not consider the problem she was facing relying on public transportation. She sometimes scolded her for coming in late. Some members also joined in spreading gossips about her coming home late onto the church compound. As the gossips continued, the pastor continued to confront her about insidious things that were being said about her.

In attempts to attract the pastor's favor toward themselves, some church members engaged in defaming others. For instance, some members in the higher echelon of the church began to ridicule Faith and other workers who lived on the church compound for the slightest mistakes they made. The nitpicking was bothersome and affected Faith's self-esteem. She felt that she was at the mercy of some of the church's elders. To add to her frustration, because the board increased her salary by five dollars more per month, some of the members complained that she was earning too much. Given her meager monthly income of thirty dollars, compounded by numerous unnecessary problems being created for her, she became despondent and lost the zeal to continue being a part of House of Faith Church.

So after some serious soul-searching, Faith informed the pastor that she was resigning from the receptionist position at the church. The pastor advised her not to leave, but the emotional burden was too unbearable for her. So she thanked the pastor for everything and left the church compound. She moved in with her girlfriend, Audrey, who had a rental room. Faith immediately began to look for a job even though she was not yet a high school graduate.

School and Work

While attending night school, Faith became friendly with a woman named Eve who was also a student there. Eve later introduced Faith to her husband, Lorenzo, and mentioned that Faith was a singer. So Lorenzo invited Faith to their church one Sunday, where she was asked to sing a song for the congregation. After she sang, everyone complimented her on how beautiful her voice was. A high-ranking government official, who was a member of Lorenzo's church, was especially impressed and commented favorably on her singing. He asked Lorenzo to bring Faith to the church again, so she could lift their spirits with her beautiful voice. Faith felt very happy about the positive reception from Lorenzo's church for her singing. This uplifted her spirit and made her feel very good about herself.

After a while, Lorenzo started referring to Faith as his God-sister. He and Eve began visiting her at Audrey's place. During one of those visits, Faith asked Lorenzo if he could help her find a job. He told her that training was taking place in two weeks at his office for radio room technicians and promised to add her name to the list of trainees. She was ecstatic and grateful for Lorenzo's ability to help her secure a job where he worked. After the training, she was hired, and it was her first civil service job. Although her monthly income was not a lot, it was, however, twice the amount she made at House of Faith Church.

After Faith started working, she rented a room in the same house where she was living with her girlfriend, Audrey. She finally had a room of her own. She eventually stopped attending House of Faith Church, and things were getting much better. As their friendship became stronger, she spent some weekends with Eve and Lorenzo. They treated her with respect, and she enjoyed their company. She also accompanied them out of town sometimes when they visited family. Their family was good to Faith, and she occasionally attended church service with them out of town. They appreciated her singing.

Meeting Mr. Liberty

One day, while at a function at Eve and Lorenzo's home, Faith was introduced to a prominent man in the community named, Mr. Liberty. He immediately struck a conversation with her.

"Do you have a boyfriend, Faith? Because I am in love with you."

"I do not know you, and you are older than me. Are you married?"

"I am divorced, and my girlfriend and I just separated. Her things are still at my house because we lived together, but she will be moving them soon. Why are you shy? I truly mean what I am saying. Can I visit you?"

"I do not know what to say because I do not know you."

"Okay, I will continue to pursue you because I love you."

Faith was afraid of going into another relationship. All she could think about was *man*, *baby*, and *suffering*. She had flashbacks about past traumatic experiences when she had both of her children. She was afraid and indecisive, but Mr. Liberty persistence eventually persuaded her to go out with him. The decision to date him was the best decision that she made in many years. Her life was dramatically changed for the better.

Feeling pleased that Faith finally agreed to date him, Mr. Liberty moved her into an apartment in the city and supplied all her needs.

In addition, he gave her extra money to treat herself to whatever she wanted. She could then buy clothes and supplies for Baby Andrew who came to spend some weekends with her. She was in love with her new apartment and new life, hoping and praying that things at least remain the same if they did not improve.

Two years later, Mr. Liberty moved Faith into his house in the suburbs of Monrovia. Her life was very good, and she was well pleased. However, still determined to further her education abroad, she had a talk with Mr. Liberty and told him that she wanted to go to the United States for school. Fortunately for her, one of her cousins named Cecelia who lived in the United States was in town for a visit. Faith talked with her about going back with her to attend school. Her cousin agreed that she could accompany her. And so Mr. Liberty being in favor of her pursuing her education, willing paid the travel expenses for her to travel with her cousin to the United States. He contributed to Faith's living expenses in her cousin's house.

After a few months of arrival in America and settling in Rhode Island, Faith registered for GED studies. She successfully passed the GED examination and received her high school diploma. Immediately afterward, she enrolled in a junior college and began taking a few remedial courses. However, after a year of living in America and studying, she unfortunately had to return to Liberia. She had to leave her cousin Cecelia apartment, because some relative moved in, and there was not enough room for everyone. In addition, the harsh winter months were difficult for her as she was often sick.

When she returned to Liberia, she moved into an apartment, and things were harder financially. So she moved back into Mr. Liberty's home, and he had her enrolled in an all-female executive secretarial school. One of the requirements to enter the school was a high school diploma. She was happy that she had obtained her GED in the United States, which enabled her to fulfill that require-ment for entry into the secretarial school. She made several friends at the school and enjoyed the learning experience and fun they had together.

Faith eventually decided to retrieve her child, Andrew, from his paternal grandmother's care to live with her at Mr. Liberty's house in the suburbs. She wanted her son to bond more with her and get to know her better. Her situation had improved, and she also wanted to be part of his development. He had now grown into boyhood. However, her decision upset Andrew's grandmother, who had taken good care of him from infancy and did not want her relationship with Andrew broken. Faith respected Andrew's grandmother's position, so she suggested an amicable compromise, time-sharing. They agreed that Andrew would alternatively spend time with each of them. During Faith's times with Andrew, she focused on his education.

Toward the end of her study at the executive secretarial school, a civil war broke out in Liberia. Unexpectedly and sadly, Mr. Liberty was arrested as a political prisoners, and Faith was terrified about his safety. There were numerous questions flooding her mind. Why did this happen to disrupt the peaceful, joyful flow of her life? She had just begun to enjoy her life with Mr. Liberty giving her the care that she so needed and longed for. Why did this dreadful incident take place to interrupt her precious relationship with Mr. Liberty? But there were no answers for these questions, including others that came to her mind.

The conditions at the prison, where Mr. Liberty was detained, were deplorable. The food was poorly prepared, and the prisoners received very little to eat each day. Worse of all, most of the prisoners, including Mr. Liberty, did not have their medications with them. So Faith and others with imprisoned family members decided to take some relief to the prisoners, even though it was risky. They resorted to befriending some of the soldiers who guarded the prisoners. As friendships with the guards became stronger, Faith and the others would ask the guards to take food and medications to their relatives and friends in prison.

While Faith was standing in a crowd during one of her prison visits, a soldier pointed to her and demanded that she follow him. She was frightened but had no choice; she had to do as the soldier ordered. The soldier told her to walk in front of him while he pointed his gun toward her back. He led her across the prison yard into the prison administrator's office. He then reported to his boss that she brought food to a political prisoner, and that he had seen her making arrangement with a soldier to take it in. He indicated that he wanted to set an example by publicly penalizing her to deter others from smuggling food and medications into the prison. And so the soldier's boss committed Faith to the women's jail. She wondered why the soldier picked her out from among all the others, who were trying to smuggle things into the prison for their family members and friends. However, she was taken aback to find out that one of the jail inmates was an influential woman, who knew Faith well. This jail matriarch, for some reasons, gave instructions that no one should bother her. Her word was a decree in jail, so all the inmates obeyed. She wondered how the matriarch knew her.

Without knowing it, Faith had helped the matriarch about a year ago at House of Faith Church. The matriarch reminded her that she was helpful to her whenever she went for spiritual counseling and prayer appointments with Pastor Bendu. During that time, the matriarch was battling certain physical and mental health challenges. As she vaguely remembered helping the matriarch, a biblical verse that she had read some years ago at House of Faith Church came to mind. It essentially states, "Be not forgetful to entertain strangers: for thereby some have entertained angels unawares" (Hebrew 13:2 KJV). The seemingly unwarranted but gladly appreciated protection she was receiving supported the spiritual truth behind this biblical verse. She was happy because her jail friend was the undisputed leader of all the women in jail. And so she felt somewhat safe because her matriarch friend was surely watching over her. She thanked God for his divine protection.

To be expected, however, Faith could not sleep well, missing the conveniences that made sleeping at night possible. There were not many beds, so some of the inmates slept on makeshift pallets on the floor made from cardboard boxes. Worse of all, the rooms were too small, and they were jammed into them. Faith prayed fervently that night that God would send someone to get her out of jail. Sooner than later, God answered her prayers.

Somehow, word of Faith's incarceration got out and reached Menan, one of Faith's dear girlfriends who lived in the city. The news upset her so much that she was moved to seek help to get Faith out of jail. Fortunately, she had some political connections that she used on Faith's behalf. Menan informed her friend who held a high-ranking position in the Liberian Army about Faith's incarceration. The next morning, Faith prayed to not spend another night in jail, and God answered her prayer. On that very day, the jail administrator had her released. She was overjoyed and thanked God and her friend, Menan, for making her release possible. After her release, she pleaded with all her friends not to let Mr. Liberty know that she was incarcerated for trying to smuggle food and medication into his prison cell. She knew that he would be disturbed by that and perhaps get sick. Also, she didn't want him overburdened; he already had a lot to worry about.

At the same time, unusual happenings around town heightened people's awareness of an impending civil uprising. As tension increased among rival forces, it became increasingly apparent and unnerving day-by-day that war was eminent, and this impacted Faith's attendance at the secretarial school. Because of her irregular attendance and lack of money to pay outstanding fees, she considered dropping out of school. But after informing the director of the school, Mrs. Coleman, about her dilemma, the director advised her not to quit or worry about the delinquent school fees. She consoled and informed Faith that she was very good friends with Mr. Liberty, and she knew he would pay the fees as soon as he was released from prison. Mrs. Coleman also assured her that she would not put her out of school because she wanted her to complete her studies and graduate at the end of the program. Grateful for Mrs. Coleman's understanding and kindness, she became energized and determined to continue working hard and attending regularly despite unsafe public conditions.

New Job

Shortly upon graduating from the secretarial school, Faith was hired by a shipping company. The pay was good, and she was happy because it was easier to afford necessities for Andrew and herself. She felt relieved and excited not to have to depend entirely on Mr. Liberty for everything. Grateful for her education and her growing economic success, a preview of how good life could be was her drive to continue learning and excelling.

In the meantime, after several months in jail, Mr. Liberty was finally released. It was clear to see how horribly he had been treated while imprisoned. His body was covered with evidence of the many beatings he had received at the hands of the soldiers. Eventually, however, he and Faith was together for six years before she got pregnant. Once again, unpleasant memories of previous pregnancies and neglect by the fathers of her children, which led to her enduring severe hardships, flooded her mind. She was afraid that those bad experiences would be repeated with her current pregnancy. So worried and depressed, she became sick as she was during her previous pregnancies, but she shortly realized that her current situation was greatly different. She was living in a home with Mr. Liberty, the father of her unborn child, providing economic, as well as emotional, stabilities. In addition, she had her own income, which gave her a sense of security as well. Regardless of these facts, she did not want any surprises. And so the thought of going back to the United States became her primary focus. She always had a strong feeling that there were some blessings waiting for her there. And in order to attain those blessings, she put her feminine charms to work and enticed Mr. Liberty to send her back to the United States.

"Where are you, my darling?" Mr. Liberty lovingly called out to Faith as soon as he entered the house after a long day at work. He was used to seeing her waiting for him on the front porch with kisses before they entered the house.

"Darling, where are you?" he called out as he moved away from the living room into the den and then into the bedroom, but he could not find Faith. He paused and listened and heard water running in the bathroom.

"Darling!" He knocked on the bathroom door three times, but she did not answer because she couldn't hear with the water running and the singing she was doing. He knocked harder the fourth, fifth, and sixth time before she finally answered.

"Yes, Li, I'm taking a shower. Want to join me?" she spoke as gracefully and as she could.

"Thanks, darling, I'll go ahead and eat my supper because I am starving."

"Okay, I will be out shortly."

While Mr. Liberty was having his dinner, Faith finished her shower and began to carefully ready herself for appealing to his most intimate senses. She got dressed in her pj's and put on his favorite perfume. And ever so gently, she applied a discrete coat of her favorite red lipstick on her lips to accentuate their fullness. After this, she stood back and examined herself in the tall floor-to-ceiling mirror in the master bathroom. She was pleased with her looks.

"Are you okay in there, Faith?" Mr. Liberty called out to her. The tone of his voice suggesting some concern.

"I'm doing fine, Li." She walked softly.

Before she could reach within an earshot of him, he turned around. The fragrance of tantalizing perfume had betrayed her presence. Mr. Liberty smelled the fragrance coming from the direction of the bedroom. He turned around, and there she was!

Taken aback, Mr. Liberty's heart skipped a couple of beats but quickly readjusted.

"Oh, darling, you look so beautiful!" He stood up away from the table and kissed her. Mr. Liberty could not believe this unexpected but much desired display of affection. He quickly doubled his steps. She also doubled her backward steps into the bedroom. He quickly entered the bedroom and slammed the door behind him. The next morning before she woke up, Mr. Liberty left a check on the dining table with a simple note, saying, "Darling, you may go ahead and buy your air ticket today. You are the best, and you deserve the best."

Although Mr. Liberty was sad to see Faith leaving him again, he, however, graciously paid for her plane ticket, gave her spending money, and sent her off to start a new life in search of her American Dreams. Faith had a strong belief that she would find stability in the United States. She reasoned that she would find a job to ultimately gain financial stability just in case Mr. Liberty stopped providing her financial assistance. She was certain that she would get ahead in the United States, and with such strong faith, she said aloud, "God bless America!"

When Faith arrived in the United States of America, she was able to rent a one-bedroom apartment and bought some necessities for the apartment, including baby furniture, using some of the money Mr. Liberty had given her. Her baby was soon to be born, and she wanted to have the room set up ahead of time. She didn't want to be homeless or dependent on others for shelter as she so often had to do in Liberia. In the meanwhile, however, Mr. Liberty continued to send her money to help with her expenses each month as she did not yet have a job.

After a few months, Faith gave birth to a bouncing healthy 8.8-pound baby girl she named Leona. She was very excited that her baby was by birth, a United States citizen. For six months, she stayed home and took care of Baby Leona before she considered searching for a job. It was her desire to become independent and able to support herself. Even though she was grateful to Mr. Liberty and felt indebted to him for being ever so kind to her, she knew that she would be able to support herself and her children once she had a job. She, therefore, solicited the help of the few people she knew in Rhode Island to help her find a job.

In addition to the stress of a job search, Faith worried about her other child, Andrew. She wanted to continue to assist with Andrew's care as she did before she moved to the United States. However, she was pleased to learn that Andrew's father, Tom, had finally assumed responsibility of his son by moving him in with him and his wife who was instrumental in this decision. And she was happy for Andrew because she knew a boy needed his father in his life. Tom was financially more capable of taking care of his son than his mother. She learned that he had enrolled Andrew in a very good school, and he was doing well in his lessons. This was what she always prayed for, for her son, that he would get the best education possible. She had given him all the support she could while in Liberia. With a strong belief in education, she had a sense of satisfaction whenever she was in school, acquiring new knowledge. And this was what she wanted for her son.

Feeling the need to continue furthering her education, Faith decided that the most important thing for her to do was to go back to school to acquire the necessary skills needed to become successful in America. She had received secretarial training in Liberia but could not operate a computer, which was necessary to perform higher-level secretarial duties in America. In her search for a secretarial job, she discovered that the jobs in this area required skills she did not have. Therefore, she knew it was necessary to go back to secretarial school if she wanted to work as a secretary. Fortunately for her, her GED certificate met the requirement for enrollment in the Philadelphia School of Office Technologies. After her studies, she graduated with an associate degree in business with concentration in executive secretarial study.

With her advanced secretarial training, Faith obtained a secretarial position in a bank. She was pleased with herself that she had acquired the education and training necessary to get a secretarial job. Mr. Liberty stopped sending her any financial help, and he asked if she could return to Liberia. Faith refused because she was in the US where she could work and earn her own money to support she and her daughter. She was happy that she completed her studies, and she had a job, so she was not so worried. Her monthly income covered her rent, utilities, and other bills. And there was enough money remaining for food and other expenses. With this level of financial security, she felt confident that she would excel in accomplishing her American Dream.

Work at the bank was hectic, and using public transportation to take her daughter, Leona, to daycare before heading to work was frustrating. This challenge was daunting for her, a single mother. And worse of all, she was often late for work. Because these challenges were becoming too much for her to manage, Faith decided it would be better to find a job working at night. She then found a job in the human services field with a better schedule. It was easier to take her child to the daycare center and pick her up using public transportation and prepare meals before going to work at night. She solicited the help of a friend to look after Leona at night for a small fee. Fortunately, her friend was empathetic with her situation and charged her less than an actual babysitting service would charge. Also, Leona slept throughout the night, and she was at her friend's place early in the morning to get her child.

Continued Education

As a human services worker, Faith's duties were a lot harder and more exhausting than the secretarial duties she performed at the bank. She soon realized that she did not want to do other people's laundry, cleaning, and taking care of people for the rest of her life. Therefore, once again, she decided that the best way out of performing such menial physical duties was through continued education. To attain the knowledge and skills for a better job with higher income, she had to go back to school. And so her next step was to attend a junior college. At first, she had to do some remedial courses before her main courses. It took several semesters. But being studious and determined, she made the dean's list, then later, the president's list. She was so elated that she was doing college courses and succeeding. Her future was already beginning to look better for a professional career.

Upon graduation from junior college with an associate degree in human services, a mental health organization hired her as a resident advisor. Her salary was higher, and she couldn't be happier. Again, she was living the American dream and accomplishing her goals. She learned several useful skills on the job, making her more confident in performing her duties. As a result, she received very good job performance evaluations.

After a few years, Faith and Leona traveled to Liberia to see Andrew. She could only afford one-way tickets, depending on Mr.

Liberty to pay for their tickets back to America after their visit. At first, she was afraid to take the chance, but her desire to see her beloved son, Andrew, prompted her to do so anyway. When they arrived in Liberia, she was so excited and happy to see Andrew, and Leona met her brother for the first time. She gave Andrew the clothes and Nintendo games she brought him, and everyone was happy.

While in Liberia, armed rebels opposing the leadership of Liberia began entering the country. She had just received her United States resident status prior to her trip. But not yet a citizen, she feared getting caught up in a horrific situation in Liberia would make it difficult leaving the country with Leona. So she appealed to Mr. Liberty to purchase their return tickets before the tense political situation worsened. She was very worried about leaving Andrew behind in Liberia with the possibility of a civil war on the horizon. His immigration application was still pending, and she couldn't wait to contact the US immigration to inquire about its status when she got back.

Upon her return to America, Faith continued to worry about Andrew and other family members in Liberia. Before she left Liberia, the rebels were not yet in Monrovia, so people were going on about their normal business. In fact, most people did not think that the situation would escalate to a full-blown civil war. However, as the political crisis began to worsen, she got more worried but was relieved when she called Andrew's stepmother who informed her that they were trying to get a visa for him to leave Liberia for America. Fortunately, a short while later, his visa was granted, and he joined his mother and sister in America. Faith eventually purchased a home so that each of her children would have a room and become a happy family. Her next task was focusing on Andrew and Leona getting quality education.

During those tumultuous years of the civil war in Liberia, Henry's mother, Ma Victoria, was fortunate to obtain an American visa to visit her daughter in Rhode Island. Although it had been several years after the death of Faith's daughter, Holly, Ma Victoria always seemed uncomfortable and regretful whenever she met Faith. She seemed to be so sad about her granddaughter's tragic death. Whereas, Faith always seemed to not be comfortable in her presence.

It was apparent that she always thought about her daughter dying at her grandmother's Ma Victoria home. She truly wanted to avoid her because seeing her brought sadness.

Some may refer to the meeting between Ma Victoria and Faith in Rhode Island one night a coincidence, but it appeared more than that. Faith and her friend, Carrie, were traveling together from Philadelphia to Rhode Island. But her actual destination was to visit some relatives in Massachusetts, which is about an hour away from Rhode Island. The plan was that her relatives would pick her up from Rhode Island since they were attending a meeting there. So she ended up with Carrie at Holly's aunt, Janet's house. Holly's grandmother Ma Victoria lived with her daughter Janet. My friend Carrie was Janet's sister in law. She was married to Carrie's brother.

While Faith was waiting for her relatives, Faith received a call from one of her family member letting her know that they had an emergency, so they could not pick her up as planned that day. Instead, they would come the next morning. And so Carrie asked Janet if Faith could spend the night with them. Of course, Ma Victoria was quick to mention that Faith was family, and she was excited to have her at their home. She told Faith that she was welcome to share her king-sized bed since it was big enough for two to sleep comfortably, but Faith was clearly taken aback by the unexpected change of events concerning her trip to visit relatives in Massachusetts. She was taken off guard because she did not expect to spend the night with Ma Victoria and her daughter in Rhode Island. Neither did she expect to be sharing a bed with her dear Ma Victoria.

To her surprise, however, that night spent at Janet's home, sharing her mother, Ma Victoria's, bed was not exactly what she expected. She did not know how the night would be because she had not seen Ma Victoria for years, but instead, they laughed and talked most of the night like mother and daughter. And she sensed that Ma Victoria wanted her to be free with her again like the past. Ma Victoria seemed very happy that day. They ultimately united again that night, and Faith appreciated the time spent. It was like old times. They promised to stay connected to keep their renewed relationship alive. Faith thanked her friend, Carrie, for taking her to Janet's home, which enabled the long overdue reconciliation.

And so when she returned home, she kept the lines of communication open between Ma Victoria and herself. She called often to check on her, and talking with her brought back many memories. Unfortunately, it was not long after Faith and Ma Victoria reconciled that she sadly passed away. Faith was happy that she was given the opportunity to sing at her funeral in Rhode Island. It was a good thing that she had connected again with Ma Victoria. Their relationship had deepened and became as strong as that of a mother and daughter's. She loved Ma Victoria and missed her dearly. Ma Victoria was a good caring woman.

Prior to Ma Victoria's death, Faith recalled communicating with Henry and encouraging him to come to America to see his mother, but he made no effort. His mother had not seen him since he left Liberia to work on the ship. She had been grieving his absence silently ever since. It had been many years since he took a job on a ship and sailed away. He had not come back to see his mother nor Faith, the mother of his first child, the woman who he was so madly in love with. Then living in Brazil, Faith called and spoke to him. Henry told Faith that he had two children who the mother had died, and that he was taking care of his children alone. In the middle of his story about his deceased's wife and motherless children, he suddenly began to cry about his baby; death. Faith encouraged him to stay strong for his other two children. She assured him that she had forgiven him and no longer had any grudge against him for leaving her to grieve the tragic death of Holly alone. Henry apologized for leaving Faith alone to grief over the death of Holly.

Although he assured Faith that he would take some time off his job to come to see his mother, he never did. But she was not in the least surprised by his broken promise. She remembered well how he told her that he would come to see her, but he never did. Ma Victoria died without ever seeing her son again. And unfortunately for him, he was unable to obtain an American visa to attend her funeral. She could not understand why Henry did not keep any of his promises. She never saw the love of her life again after he left to work on a ship. Because surprisingly, not long after his mother's death, he died. And regardless of her not seeing him for so many years, she grieved his death. Reminiscing, she recalled that he came into her life when she was down and had nothing. He took over her care despite his meager income. She was thankful that she had talked with him on the telephone when she tried to persuade him to come and see his mother. Somehow, she managed to put those bitter memories of difficult years behind her and looked faithfully to a better life in the United States of America.

Faith's American Dream

Faith always believed that education was the key to a successful life. This belief fostered very early in her life when she lived with her cousins, Mama and Dada, who had reared her from childhood into her early teens. They taught and practiced good moral values in their home and instilled those values in their own children, as well as those in their care.

Given the fact that they priced education highly, she never understood why Mama and Dada did not send her to boarding school along with Budu. Since they never gave her any explanation for their decision, she gradually reached some reasonable conclusions about this matter later in life. She reasoned that Mama and Dada probably waited for her father to shoulder the financial responsibilities of boarding school for his daughter. Her father may have paid her boarding school expenses if he had advance notice. However, he seldom left his farm to visit her at Mama and Dada because it was located many miles away in a distant town. Now she was accepting that she would never know the true reason why she was not afforded the opportunity of boarding school to continue her education. These were just some of the possibilities she came up with, but she also knew that her curiosity about the truth of this matter would always puzzle her.

And so because this matter continued to plague her after such a long time and because nothing she could come up with seemed rational, she continued to revisit it from time to time... Perhaps if she had waited for her father to come from his farm instead of packing her bags and leaving Mama and Dada, he would have sent her to a boarding school since he had the financial means to do so. But she was not mature enough to put things into proper perspective being a young teen. And Mama and Dada's silence about the matter did not give her any assurance to put her mind at ease. She reasoned further that maybe Mama and Dada had to bear the full financial burden of their grandson, Budu, for boarding school and couldn't afford hers. Another possibility she probably was not aware of was that Budu could have received a scholarship from the Episcopal Church because of his role as an altar boy. The reality was she was too young to think reasonably about Mama and Dada's decision, not to let her accompany Budu to boarding school, along with all her peers. The only thing she could think about at the time was that Budu and all her friends were leaving home for junior high school in Harper, except her. She always remembered how she felt when she learned that she would not be going and how Mama and Dada's failure to explain why they did not help her. As a young child, the experience was very devastating and left her feeling ridiculed throughout her life. Now that she was older and knowledgeable about some facts of life and especially how not having enough money could affect major life's decisions, she felt empathetic about Mama and Dada's situation. It had to be a difficult decision for them since they had always treated her as their own child, never showing any difference between Budu and her. It was time to forgive and move on.

It eventually dawned on Faith that Mama and Dada had also had suffered some regrets about the matter. They knew that most of the young graduates from elementary school, including her, were anxiously looking forward to leaving home to attend junior high school in Harper. So looking back, she knew they were very much aware of how devastated she was when she realized that she wouldn't be leaving for Harper. However, she acknowledged their efforts in her upbringing and was grateful to them for instilling in her the value of education as a very young child. This was the basis of her belief that teaching young children good values was crucial for character-building, which led to them embracing those values throughout their lifetime.

Finally, Faith reverted her thoughts from her childhood and began reflecting on higher education goals.

After graduation, Faith applied for a job with a health care system and was hired as a support coordinator/case manager. Being a position of esteem, her coworkers regarded her highly, and she began to realize her value and obligations to her job. More importantly, her income far exceeded that of her previous job. She was amazed how much her life had transformed from a struggling young girl who barely had food to eat a few year ago to an executive employee of a major organization, now enjoying a better life due to a new job with a great salary. But to Faith, the icing on the cake was the elaborate employee education policy that the organization had. While reviewing the employee handbook, she discovered that her employer would pay a large percentage for employees who wanted to further their education.

Learning about her employer's contribution to education, Faith immediately decided to take advantage of it. She enrolled at an accredited college in Philadelphia and obtained a bachelor's in human services.

After completing her program of study, she felt indebted to her employer for the opportunity to increase her learning. At this point, she felt academically complete. Her confidence grew as she realized how much she was contributing to the success of her employer. Considering her leadership potential and success, she knew she had reached her zenith—living the American dream!

On her vacations to Liberia, Faith often met children who lack proper education. In empathy with their situation, she decided to pursue her master's in education. It was her intention to return to Liberia one day to contribute to educating Liberia's children. So upon her return to the United States, she enrolled at an accredited University in Philadelphia. The courses were very difficult probably because she was older, and her comprehension skills were not as sharp. It meant she had to spend more time studying and staying up late to complete schoolwork. One requirement for graduation, however, was to complete a three-month internship of teaching. She was worried about this because she did not have enough money saved to take a leave of absence for three months without pay. Also, at this time, rumors were spreading that the company was about to engage in massive layoffs.

Three months before Faith was supposed to start teaching, her supervisor told her that she would be laid-off from her job. This was something that was expected. Faith's contract was for a year, and it lasted five years. Fortunately for her, she received her full salary and benefits until she graduated from University. *This is the American dream*, she thought, *being laid-off with pay and benefits for six months!* It was enough time for her to accomplish her goal, and she could hardly believe her good fortune.

So three months after Faith graduated from the University with a master's in education, she went on a vacation to Liberia. While there, she received an invitation to deliver the keynote address to graduates of Caine High School. She ascended the stage, walked to the podium, stood and surveyed the audience silently for a moment.

As she carefully fought the surge of emotions that welled up in her heart, she spoke extemporaneously, "Forty years ago, I could not complete my high school education here in Liberia due to abject poverty. My father died when I was a young lady, and my mother could not afford to send me to high school. Although some of my relatives had the means to assist with my schooling, they chose not to, but I held fast to my dream that one day, I would travel to America and earn an advanced degree. I eventually went to America, and after overcoming many obstacles, I ultimately earned a master's degree.

"You may wonder how I did it…someone who was hungry with no food to eat and, at one point, homeless in Monrovia to succeed in the United States of America? Let me share with you four ingredients of my seemingly impossible success. First, I cultivated an unwavering faith that all things are possible for those who believe in God. Second, I kept a clear vision in mind of the major things I desired to achieve in my life. Third, I held onto my dream with a bulldog-type of tenacity. During severe hardships, disappointments, and frustrations, I never let go my dream. And fourth, I adopted a spiritual mantra, which I repeated to myself several times a week, 'I returned, and saw under the sun, that the race is not to the swift, nor the battle to the strong, neither yet bread to the wise, nor yet riches to men of understanding, not yet favour to of skill; but time and chance happeneth to them all' [Ecclesiastes 9:11 (KJV)].

"I, therefore, challenge you, honorable graduating class, to do the following—believe steadfastly in God, even in the face of apparent impossibilities, clearly visualize your dreams, hold fast onto your vision with a bulldog-type of tenacity regardless of naysayers and disappointments. Finally, encourage yourselves when the going gets tough by saying to yourselves, 'I can do all things through Christ which strengthens me' [Philippians 4:13 (KJV)].

"If you dared to do these four things, my friends, you too will achieve your dreams someday. Thank you."

About the Author

Mai C. Stevens is an educator who lives and works in Philadelphia, Pennsylvania. Without a high school education, she migrated from Liberia, West Africa, to the United States of America in pursuit of her long-cherished American Dream. She accomplished her dream by working diligently at various odd jobs to sustain her children and herself while pursuing her education and keeping her eyes on her vision. Eventually, she obtained an associate degree in human services from  Camden County College, a bachelor's degree in human services from Chestnut Hill College, a master's degree in human services from Lincoln University, and a master's degree in education from Saint Joseph's University. In addition, as a talented Gospel singer, she enjoys singing at family and friends' events. She is a devout Christian who strongly believes that all things are possible with God. And even amid hardships, she is steadfast in that belief and trusts in the Creator to carry her through all challenges. With her dreams being realized, her life continues to flourish day by day.

CPSIA information can be obtained
at www.ICGtesting.com
Printed in the USA
LVHW021958140821
695337LV00003B/474